Development Projects
Observed

ALBERT O. HIRSCHMAN

Development Projects Observed

THE BROOKINGS INSTITUTION
Washington, D.C.

About Brookings

The Brookings Institution is a private nonprofit organization devoted to research, education, and publication on important issues of domestic and foreign policy. Its principal purpose is to bring knowledge to bear on current and emerging policy problems. The Institution was founded in December 1927 to merge the activities of the Institute for Government Research, founded in 1916, the Institute of Economics, founded in 1922, and the Robert Brookings Graduate School of Economics, founded in 1924.

The Institution maintains a position of neutrality on issues of public policy. Interpretations or conclusions in Brookings publications should be understood to be solely those of the authors.

Contents

Author's Preface:
A Hidden Ambition

WHEN, IN 1966, I DELIVERED the manuscript of this book to the Brookings Institution I experienced the relief and satisfaction we normally feel when we manage to complete a book with particular intensity. The reason is that, at least in my more exalted moments, I saw this book as the final volume of a "trilogy": in *The Strategy of Economic Development*, I had attempted to understand some basic processes making for economic progress in the developing countries;[1] the corresponding political processes were then explored in *Journeys toward Progress*;[2] and, after having concentrated in these two books on the macro aspects of development, my attention shifted in the present volume to the analysis of individual development projects, those "privileged particles of the development process" (p. 1) dealing with the construction and maintenance of highways, electric power stations, irrigation schemes, and similar specific investment activities.

These books were also held together by another progression: *Strategy* was based almost entirely on my experiences in Colombia, where I had lived from 1952 to 1956; to write *Journeys* I returned to Colombia but also studied other Latin American countries, particularly Brazil and Chile; with *Development*

1. *The Strategy of Economic Development* (Yale University Press, 1958).
2. *Journeys toward Progress: Studies of Economic Policy-Making in Latin America* (New York: Twentieth Century Fund, 1963).

vii

Projects Observed, I extended my range from Latin America (El Salvador, Ecuador, Peru, Uruguay) to Southern Europe (Italy) and to some major countries of Asia (India, Pakistan, Thailand) and Africa (Nigeria, Ethiopia).

The three books were of course conceived consecutively. The concept — or fantasy — of a unified "trilogy" emerged in my mind primarily during the writing of the present book. Over and above the overt purpose of my work — the analysis of development and the advice on policy — I came to see it as having the latent, hidden, but overriding common intent to celebrate, to "sing" the epic adventure of development — its challenge, drama, and grandeur.

The subject matter of the present book lent itself particularly well to this hidden ambition. While visiting the projects and talking to their administrators and other interested parties, I collected so many fascinating stories that storytelling came at times to overshadow analysis. At the same time there was, as one might expect, a tension between the overt task and the concealed ambition of my writing, a tension that became particularly apparent in the case of the present book. At a certain level the ex ante choice among investment projects and the ex post evaluation of success or failure deal with matters that should permit straightforward technical treatment. Moreover, when I wrote this book in the middle 1960s, the scientific determination of correct investment choices seemed to be within reach. In the U.S. Department of Defense, under the leadership of Robert McNamara and his "whiz kids," much was made of new methods of allocating available funds to various purposes. These methods were given a technocratic aura by the invention of an acronym, PPBS (planning, programming, and budgeting system), that soon acquired a considerable prestige. In the World Bank, investment choices and decisions were similarly expected to be made more rational through various devices known as "shadow prices," "social benefit cost analysis," and other sophisticated new techniques. In this intellectual atmosphere, it was to act as something of a spoilsport to call attention to very different, and much more problematic, levels of concern about projects: to speculate, for example, about the question of road versus rail construction in the light of interethnic conflict in Nigeria (where a savage civil war pitting Ibos against non-Ibos was actually to break out in 1967) or about the conceivable impact of an irrigation scheme on the pursuit of land reform in Peru.

I will admit that to give pride of place to "The Principle of the Hiding Hand," the most speculative chapter of the book, was close to a provocation. Nothing could be less "operationally useful" than to be told that underestimating the costs or difficulties of a project has on occasion been helpful in eliciting creative energies that otherwise might never have been forthcoming. The stories told in this first chapter of the book were of course not meant to hold any immediately applicable "practical" lesson. Yet they did have a purpose closely connected with my hidden agenda: to endow and surround the development story with a sense of wonder and mystery that would reveal it to have much in common with the highest quests undertaken by humankind.

The first chapter on the hiding hand was actually meant to function as a prologue, somewhat removed from the rest of the book. The subsequent chapters deal with more mundane aspects of construction and operation of projects, and here I do come forward, particularly in the chapters on "Uncertainties" and on "Latitudes and Disciplines," with a number of useful hints, suggestions, and propositions. Many of my generalizations about the behavior of development projects have their origin in the peculiar lenses I had formed in the course of my previous writing on development. For example, the concept of "latitude for poor performance" had played a considerable role in *Strategy*. In chapter 8 of that book, I suggested that less developed countries may have a comparative advantage in tasks — such as the running of airlines — where this latitude is narrow, rather than in tasks — such as the building and maintenance of highways — where latitude is wide. In the latter tasks, developing countries would tend to gravitate toward the poor end of the performance scale, in contrast to situations where the nature of the task would oblige them to do well.

This basic idea helped to cast light on various aspects of the projects I studied. Projects whose latitude is limited by being "site-bound" (pp. 87–95) or whose construction is "time-bound" (pp. 95–103) were duly shown to have a number of advantages over those that do not exhibit these characteristics. Parenthetically I may note here that time-boundedness and narrow latitude for performance in general are close relatives of the "just-in-time" technique that has become well known as a key feature of Japanese industrial production methods.

Fortunately the present book did not limit itself to "applying" ideas already laid out in *Strategy*. Although I did not say so — for the good reason that I did not become aware of it — I encountered in some of the projects I studied the limits of the validity and applicability of the theorem that laid down the rule "the less latitude the better." This rule had been developed primarily with regard to technology. As I put it later: "a certain type of capital-intensive, advanced technology could be more appropriate, in a country with little industrial tradition, than ... labor-intensive technology and 'idiot-proof' machinery."[3] But in the present book, I looked beyond technology at the social and cultural environment in which development projects come to be embedded. In the process I realized that it may not always be possible to effect a radical transformation of this environment by the mere injection of some development project that requires such a transformation in order to succeed.

3. "A Dissenter's Confession," in *Rival Views of Market Society and Other Recent Essays* (Viking, 1986), pp. 18–19.

In chapter 4, I distinguished therefore between projects that are "trait-taking" and others that are "trait-making," in analogy to price theory, where the distinction between price taking (in competition) and price making (in conditions of monopoly or oligopoly) had long played an important role. "Trait-taking" stood for situations where a project fits easily into a given social and cultural structure and does not attempt to modify it, whereas a trait-making project is more ambitious: it must change some aspect of that structure somewhere if it is going to be successful. Using this distinction, I could show, for example, that highways that "run themselves" through individually owned trucks are trait-taking: they fitted far better into the existing multiethnic structure and rivalries of Nigeria than the trait-making railroads with their centralized bureaucracy, which, against all probability, was supposed to be tribe-blind and staffed along strictly meritocratic lines.

In the end, my argument amounted to denouncing attempts at trait-making under certain conditions. Some narrow-latitude tasks simply go beyond the capacity of a society as presently constituted and are therefore likely to end in failure. In other words, without realizing it at the time I had come up against the limits of one of my most cherished insights.

In recent years I have passed through several experiences of arguing against earlier propositions of mine because I noted that they were less general than I originally thought. I have talked about these experiences as "self-subversive" acts and eventually discussed them — and their uses — in a chapter under the heading "A Propensity to Self-Subversion."[4] This is also the title for my next book of essays.[5]

When I wrote the present book in the 1960s, I was busily

4. Lloyd Rodwin and Donald A. Schon, eds., *Rethinking the Development Experience: Essays Provoked by the Work of Albert O. Hirschman* (Brookings, 1994), chap. 12.

5. *A Propensity to Self-Subversion* (Harvard University Press, forthcoming).

building up my edifice of propositions about development and self-subversion was far from my mind. Nevertheless, I was troubled by the finding that trait-making was not functioning properly in Nigeria, that the railways did so poorly in spite of the fact that their latitude for performance was narrow. In looking for the reason I eventually focused on a paradoxical question: could it be that the increasing availability of highway transportation was depriving the railroads of the criticism (or "voice") they would have been subject to if their major customers had not had this easy alternative (or "exit") open to them (pp. 146–47)? This thought turned out to have manifold implications: it was the origin of my next book, *Exit, Voice, and Loyalty*, as I pointed out in that book's preface.[6]

In this manner, the present book was not only the last volume of my "trilogy" on development but became the bridge to the broader social science themes of my subsequent writings.

November 1994

6. *Exit, Voice, and Loyalty: Responses to Decline in Firms, Organizations, and States* (Harvard University Press, 1970).

Foreword

THE EXPERIENCE ACCUMULATED in the wake of more than two decades of sustained effort to promote growth and change in the low-income countries presents a rich field for scholarly inquiry and new insights into the development process. The Brookings Institution, which has become increasingly involved in research on economic, social, and political development, has sought in various ways to make these new materials available to the public and the policy makers. When Albert O. Hirschman expressed interest in conducting a study of selected capital assistance projects financed by the World Bank, the Institution responded promptly to the opportunity presented.

The successes and failures of such projects, the new skills and attitudes they impart, and the internal tensions they sometimes generate obviously have an important bearing on the next stages of a country's development effort. Yet little has become known about these truly formative experiences which are due to the behavior—and misbehavior—of development projects.

Professor Hirschman's well-known books, *The Strategy of Economic Development* (1958) and *Journeys Toward Progress* (1963), dealt with the circumstances under which successful development decisions, whether in the sphere of capital investment, or in the wider area of economic policy making, are most likely to emerge from initial and apparently pervasive backwardness. In the present volume, Professor

xiii

Hirschman turns his attention to the ways in which decision making is molded, activated, or hampered by the specific nature of the project that is undertaken—the establishment and operation of a pulp and paper mill in East Pakistan, an irrigation project in Peru, railway expansion in Nigeria, and other development undertakings. In some parts of the present inquiry Professor Hirschman elaborates on his earlier writings; occasionally, he qualifies or modifies his previous conclusions; the bulk of the study explores new territory.

Although the projects observed were World Bank projects—enterprises assisted financially and otherwise by the International Bank for Reconstruction and Development—the Bank bears no responsibility for the views expressed and the conclusions reached. Its role was nevertheless crucial in making the study possible. The Bank allowed the author to interview staff members, helped him contact borrowers, provided him with essential information, and in many other ways facilitated his research.

A grant from the Carnegie Corporation to the Brookings Institution financed the author's travel and research expenses. The project was planned while he was Professor of International Economic Relations at Columbia University; it was originally envisaged in connection with a year of sabbatical leave. When he was appointed at Harvard University in 1964, where he is Lucius N. Littauer Professor of Political Economy, that institution cooperated generously in granting leave. A Faculty Fellowship, provided by the Ford Foundation, was of considerable assistance to him in the summer and fall of 1964. To these institutions, Professor Hirschman and Brookings are sincerely grateful.

The members of the Brookings advisory committee established to assist the author were: John H. Adler, Robert E. Asher, Richard H. Demuth, Isaiah Frank, H. Field Haviland, Jr., Lawrence B. Krause, Edward S. Mason, Richard E.

Neustadt, John N. Plank, Walter S. Salant, and Thomas C. Schelling. Their many constructive comments on the draft manuscript are greatly appreciated. Four members—Adler, Frank, Mason, and Salant—served also as readers of the revised manuscript. The project was carried out under the general supervision of H. Field Haviland, Jr., Director of Foreign Policy Studies at Brookings. Final editing was the responsibility of Alice M. Carroll. Helen B. Eisenhart prepared the index. The Institution is grateful also to those mentioned in the Author's Acknowledgments.

Professor Hirschman contributed to another Brookings book, *Development of the Emerging Countries: An Agenda for Research*, published in 1962. An abbreviated version of the first chapter of the present volume appeared in the Winter 1967 issue of *The Public Interest*.

The views expressed in the text are those of the author and do not necessarily represent the opinions of those consulted during the course of his research. Neither should they be construed as reflecting the views of the trustees, the officers, or staff members of the Brookings Institution, the Ford Foundation, or the Carnegie Corporation.

KERMIT GORDON

President

July 1967
Washington, D.C.

Author's Acknowledgments

IN EXPRESSING MY GRATITUDE to the persons, institutions, and foundations named in the Foreword, I should like to make special mention of the Brookings Institution itself and of J. Burke Knapp, Vice President of the International Bank for Reconstruction and Development, because of their hospitality to my initial proposals concerning the present study. Subsequently, my principal obligation was incurred toward the officials, administrators, economists, and engineers who, in 1964–65, received me and my wife in the countries in which the projects we visited were located, and who arranged for field trips and gave generously of their time in frank and searching discussions.

My wife participated actively in the predeparture research and in the interviews, and on our trips she kept a diary which, together with her extensive interview notes, proved invaluable in the course of writing. In India, Shinji Asanuma of the World Bank accompanied us and provided able assistance in research and interviewing.

The manuscript was largely written in New York between February and July 1966. During this period, I profited greatly from exchanging ideas and draft chapters with Judith Tendler who was then writing her doctoral dissertation on electric power in Brazil. Miss Tendler's fine insights into the differential characteristics and side-effects of thermal and hydropower, and of generation and distribution, contributed in many ways to the formation of my views.

For reviewing the completed manuscript my greatest debt is to Charles E. Lindblom of Yale University who, once again, displayed his generosity and critical acumen by sending me extraordinarily detailed and always incisive comments. Many excellent suggestions were also received from Kenneth Bohr, Benjamin King, and Alexander Stevenson of the World Bank; from Otto Eckstein of Harvard University and Nathan Rosenberg of Purdue University; and from Walter S. Salant of the Brookings Institution. As my principal contact at Brookings, Robert E. Asher was remarkably understanding, helpful, and efficient during the entire undertaking.

ALBERT O. HIRSCHMAN

April 1967

Introduction

THE DEVELOPMENT PROJECT is a special kind of investment. The term connotes purposefulness, some minimum size, a specific location, the introduction of something qualitatively new, and the expectation that a sequence of further development moves will be set in motion. If they are in the public sector, development projects may additionally be defined as those units or aggregates of public investment that, however small, still evoke direct involvement by high, usually the highest, political authorities. Development projects, then, are privileged particles of the development process, and the feeling that their behavior warrants watching at close range led to the present inquiry.

I chose to study a number of projects financed by the International Bank for Reconstruction and Development (World Bank) whose twenty-year experience in appraising, financing, and following up development projects constitutes the most ample, varied, and detailed source of information and documentation in this area. Considering my particular purpose, which was to learn something about project behavior in general, exclusive reliance on World Bank projects could of course be criticized on the grounds that the resulting sample was likely to be highly biased because the Bank insists on very high standards and picks only the best ventures available. Fortunately (at least for my research!) I found, upon looking more closely, that not one of the projects I had selected had been free from serious problems. It quickly became apparent to me that all projects are problem-ridden; the only valid distinction

1

TABLE 1. *World Bank Projects Studied*

Country & Sector	Location or Purpose	Agency in Charge
EL SALVADOR Electric power	Hydrostation on Rio Lempa	Comisión Ejecutiva Hidroeléctrica del Rio Lempa
ECUADOR Highways	Guayas Province	Comité Ejecutivo de Vialidad de la Provincia del Guayas
PERU Irrigation	San Lorenzo Project in northern Peru	Irrigación y Colonización "San Lorenzo"
URUGUAY Livestock	Countrywide pasture improvement	Comisión Honoraria del Plan Agropecuario
INDIA Multipurpose river valley development	Damodar Valley in states of Bihar and West Bengal	Damodar Valley Corporation
PAKISTAN Industry	Pulp and paper mill on Karnaphuli River in East Pakistan	Pakistan Industrial Development Corporation, later Dawood Group
THAILAND Irrigation	Chao Phya River (Central Plain)	Royal Irrigation Department
ITALY Irrigation	Various irrigation projects in southern Italy	Cassa per il Mezzogiorno
UGANDA Electric power	Transmission and distribution from Owen Falls Station	Uganda Electricity Board
ETHIOPIA Telecommunications	Countrywide	Imperial Board for Telecommunications of Ethiopia
NIGERIA Railways	Modernization and 300-mile Bornu extension	Nigerian Railway Corporation

appears to be between those that are more or less successful in overcoming their troubles and those that are not.

With the help of the staff of the World Bank, I put together a small sample of projects on the basis of two criteria: as a group, they had to be well diversified with respect to economic sector and geographical area, and each project had to have an extended history, including if at all possible several years of operation. The latter condition limited the sample in practice to projects to which the Bank had given support at an early stage of its own operations. This should be borne in mind in connection with any critical points that will be raised here about project planning and implementation.

The study of the project histories, including frequently the portions prior or subsequent to Bank involvement, proceeded in 1964–65, first at Bank headquarters in Washington and then mainly in the field where I spent from two to five weeks per project. Eleven projects were studied and visited, in the order shown in Table 1.

In spite of this intensive concern with "cases," the study does not contain histories of the individual projects nor detailed comparisons of cost and benefit estimates with results. Rather, I have woven significant bits of the project histories into observations on project behavior that I have attempted to present in systematic form. It will, I hope, be apparent that almost all of these observations owe their very existence to a year of looking at projects and talking about them with their originators, builders, administrators, financiers, and customers. Immersion in the particular proved, as usual, essential for the catching of anything general, with the immersion-catch ratio varying of course considerably from one project to another. For a number of them, a reasonably full, if dispersed, profile will in fact have been drawn by the end of the book.

What is the nature of the catch? For my previous book, *Journeys Toward Progress*, I had studied simultaneously the histories of three different problems—inflation in Chile, land tenure in Colombia, and regional imbalance in Brazil—in order to identify some characteristic features of the policy-making and problem-solving process. This time I decided to observe in rapid succession the course of development projects in diverse economic sectors—irrigation, electric power, transportation, basic industry, etc.—with the thought that in this fashion significant similarities and differences in project experience would stand out sharply and would suggest some hypotheses on comparative project behavior. My purpose was not to establish for all projects general propositions that would almost certainly be empty, but to inquire whether significantly different experiences with projects might be traced to what, for want of a better term, may be called their "structural characteristics." These range from economic and technological attributes (for example, the extent to which it is possible to substitute labor for capital or quantity for quality in construction) to organizational or administrative properties (for example, the organization that builds the project may also be in charge of operating it, as is typically the case in railways, but not in highways which are "operated" by independent truck owners). As a result of such characteristics some projects make greater implicit demands on human effort and on the sociopolitical environment than others. For example, some projects require technological innovation while others could not hope to succeed without lessening, at least within their own confines, racial, religious, or other hostilities among various sections of the community. To view project behavior as rooted in such structural characteristics and in the interaction between those characteristics and society at large should make a two-fold contribution to our understanding.

First and principally, it should go far in explaining and anticipating successes and failures of projects, systematic veerings from pre-assigned paths, propensities toward specific difficulties, as well as opportunities for special payoffs.

Secondly and more ambitiously, this analysis of likely behavior of projects possessed of different structural characteristics inevitably leads one to viewing the development experience of a country as importantly influenced by the kind of projects it finds—or places—in its path. Such a view stresses the importance for development of what a country does and of what it becomes as a result of what it does, and thereby contests the primacy of what it is, that is, of its geography- and history-determined endowment with natural resources, values, institutions, social and political structure, etc.

This view is appealing because it affords hope to a country with the "wrong" endowment provided only it finds the "right" projects, and also because it may explain the substantial differences in development performance for not too differently endowed countries. Along these lines, it can be shown that some projects and technologies have a special vocation for inducing certain types of learning, attitude change, and institutional reform (and not others), that different projects—because of their different structural characteristics—are, as it were, specialized with respect to the kind of changes they will work. An inquiry into this nexus offers perhaps a way out of the inconclusive debate about values versus institutions as prime movers in social change and modernization.

But I hasten to say that only very occasionally—see in particular pages 128–39—have I ventured onto such lofty ground. On the whole, my energies were absorbed by the task of describing, with the help of my project sample, the principal structural characteristics of which I had become aware. While I was pleased to be able to arrange them neatly under the two headings of uncertainties (Chapter 2) and latitudes or disciplines (Chapter 3), I became at times concerned over their number and variety—in other words, over the very success of my search. If every one of these characteristics can claim to inflect project behavior in some way, are we then not back at that "chaos of causes" about which Herder complained after he had improved upon Montesquieu's stress on climate as the principal determinant of differences among human societies, by asking that account be also taken of "the food and drink which man takes in, the way he lives, the work he performs ... and a multitude of other circumstances"?[1]

Nevertheless, at the risk of rendering the universe less, rather than more, intelligible, my first duty clearly was to map out as fully as possible the territory I had chosen as my field of investigation. Considering the smallness of the sample from which I have extracted my "system," it seems likely that additional important connections between the technical or economic characteristics of projects and their performance in different sociopolitical environments remain to be recognized. Insofar as the categories here proposed are concerned, their large number should make for less "chaos" than might be feared: they are meant for selective use, rather than for mechanical application all the way through to any and every project. For this reason and also to avoid the illusion of completeness, I have resisted the temptation to append an elaborate checklist of criteria.

From what has been said, it is clear that Chapters 2 and 3 on uncertainties and latitudes are central to my argument. They are followed by attempts to develop the bearing of the resulting notions on project design (Chapter 4) and project appraisal (Chapter 5).

This leaves Chapter 1 to be accounted for. Essentially it is an attempt to answer a question that is preliminary and fundamental to the rest of the inquiry: if it is true that progressive

---

1. *Ideen zur Philosophie der Geschichte der Menschheit*, Pt. 2, Bk. 7, in *Herder's Werke* (Berlin: Hempel, 1879), Vol. 10, pp. 51, 62.

change can assert itself in a country simply as a result of what that country does and in spite of many things it is, what except accidental stumbling makes countries engage upon such doings in the first place? This sort of inquiry is of course a few notches more speculative than the rest of the book. Meant originally as a prologue, it should be read as such.

Having set out the principal focus of the present study, I should perhaps caution the reader that some of the issues he may expect to be treated in a book on development projects receive scant attention here. In the first place, very little will be said about cost-benefit analysis, shadow prices, the rate of interest appropriate for discounting, and similar topics; only in the last chapter is some space devoted to them, in connection with a discussion of so-called indirect effects or side-effects. My silence on these matters does not mean that I advocate shelving, say, the discounted cash flow technique in favor of the concepts I have derived from the observation of the behavior and misbehavior of past projects. I do expect these concepts to have some uses in project evaluation, but almost entirely as additional elements of judgment; in the few cases in which they involve a qualification or critique of traditional appraisal techniques, this is expressly noted.

Secondly, and as already mentioned, I have been less interested in achieving an overall appraisal of the individual World-Bank-financed projects I visited than in drawing on specific segments and sequences of the project histories for a more general understanding of project behavior. Hence, no special effort has been made to add up the costs and benefits of the individual projects and to rank them along a scale that would measure their overall financial or economic results. While such a comprehensive audit or reappraisal is not impossible, and while it would cater to our consuming curiosity about rank and rankings, it is not likely to be particularly useful in refining one's judgment about new projects. A new project, besides containing entirely new elements, is always a mosaic of situations characteristic of various past projects. Decomposition of project experience into various elements will therefore provide more guidance than a synthetic judgment on past projects—each of which represents a combination of elements far more unique than the component elements themselves.

More generally, the commissions and omissions of this book imply a judgment that there is far more to project evaluation than any ranking on a one-dimensional scale can convey. That this is so is of course well recognized. But the generally accepted notion appears to be that decision making on projects involves two, and only two, wholly distinct activities: ascertaining the rate of return and, then, applying feel, instinct, "seat-of-the-pants" judgment, and the like. In actual fact, these latter categories have been left to control a very large portion of the decision-making process. Rather than as a criticism of cost-benefit analysis and the rate of return, this book should be regarded as an attempt to reclaim at least part of this vast domain of intuitive discretion for the usual processes of the *raison raisonnante*.

CHAPTER ONE

The Principle of the Hiding Hand

THE KARNAPHULI pulp and paper mill is one of the earliest large-scale industrial enterprises to have been set up in Pakistan after Partition and Independence. Planned by the official Industrial Development Corporation to utilize the vast resources of the bamboo forests of the Chittagong Hill Tracts along the upper reaches of the Karnaphuli River in East Pakistan, the mill started to operate in 1953. It had perhaps more than its share of technical and managerial teething troubles, but considerable progress had been achieved by 1959 when its management passed into private hands. Soon thereafter, a major upset endangered the very life of the mill: the bamboo began to flower, an event entirely unforeseen and probably unforeseeable in the present state of our knowledge since it occurs only once every fifty to seventy years: given the resulting paucity of observations, the life cycle of the many varieties of bamboo is by no means fully known. In any event, the variety that supplied the Karnaphuli mill with some 85 percent of its raw material flowered and then, poetically but quite uneconomically, died.

It was known that flowering of the bamboo results in death of the whole plant and in regeneration from the seeds rather than, as normally, from the rhizomes; but it was *not* known that the bamboo that dies upon flowering would be unusable for pulping since it would disintegrate upon being transported and floated down the river. Another unpleasant surprise was

9

the discovery that, once flowering was over, a number of years would have to pass before the new bamboo shoots would grow to a size fit for commercial exploitation. In its seventh year of operation the mill therefore faced the extraordinary task of finding another raw material base.

In a temporary and costly way, the problem was solved by importing pulp, but other, more creative responses were not long in coming. An organization was set up to collect bamboo in villages throughout East Pakistan (the waterways crisscrossing the country make for cheap transportation of bulky cargo), sundry lumber was cut in the tracts, and, most important, a research program was started to identify other fast-growing species that might to some extent replace the unreliable bamboo as the principal raw material base for the mill. Permission was obtained to plant an experimental area of six square miles with several of the more promising species, and plans to cover a much larger area are underway. Thus, the crisis of the flowering bamboo may in the end lead to a diversification of the raw material base for the mill.

Looking backward it may be said that the Karnaphuli mill was "lucky": its planners had badly overestimated the permanent availability of bamboo, but the mill escaped the possibly disastrous consequences of this error by an offsetting underestimate—or, more correctly, by the unsuspected availability —of alternative raw materials.

The question I wish to explore is whether this experience really was a matter of pure luck or whether there are reasons to expect some systematic association of such providentially offsetting errors. A similar phenomenon often occurs in successful irrigation and irrigation-hydroelectric projects: the river that is being tapped is frequently found not to have enough water for all the power, agricultural, industrial, and urban uses that had been planned or that are staking claims, but the resulting shortage can then often be remedied by drawing on other sources that had not been within the horizon of the planners: ground water can be lifted by tubewells, the river flow can be better regulated through upstream dams, or the water of more distant rivers can be diverted. At present such plans are afoot for the San Lorenzo irrigation scheme in Peru, and for the Damodar Valley in India, among our projects; a similar overestimate of the waters available from the to-be-harnessed river which can, however, be corrected by "newly discovered" water from other rivers and areas has been reported for the Bhakra Nangal project in India "though no specific provision was made in the project for the investment on this account."[1]

It would obviously be silly to expect that overestimates of the availability of a given material resource are always going to be offset by underestimates of alternative or substitute resources; but if we generalize a little more, we obtain a statement that no longer sounds wholly absurd: on the contrary, it is quite plausible and almost trite to state that each project comes into the world accompanied by two sets of partially or wholly offsetting potential developments: (1) a set of possible and unsuspected threats to its profitability and existence, and (2) a set of unsuspected remedial actions that can be taken should a threat become real.

The experience of several of the projects visited fits this very broad proposition. For example, the San Lorenzo irrigation project in northern Peru suffered serious, and at times exasperating, delays caused by political change and second thoughts on the kind of irrigation farming the project should promote. But the considerable economic losses implied by the delays were in part offset by the fact that, as a result of the second thoughts, the San Lorenzo irrigation eventually became a pilot

1. K. N. Raj, *Some Economic Aspects of the Bhakra Nangal Project* (Asia Publishing House, 1960), pp. 53, 58.

project for the subdivision of land into small but viable family farms and for the granting of credit and technical assistance to previously landless farmers. The project thus set an entirely new pattern for Peruvian agriculture and turned unexpectedly into a breeding ground for administrators who could apply elsewhere in Peru the lessons learned in San Lorenzo.

The Uruguayan livestock and pasture improvement project also experienced extraordinary delays, first because of slowness in political and administrative decision making and then because the key technical task of improving the natural grasslands by introduction of legumes into the soil turned out to be unexpectedly complex. Yet the solutions that were gradually found through scientific research and practical experimentation and were then applied over an expanding area have now tarted to make this program into a particularly successful operation and have served to spread the spirit of innovation among a large group of Uruguayan farmers.

Somewhat similar sequences can be found in other projects, although the experience of the Nigerian Railway Corporation serves as an emphatic warning that by itself trouble does not constitute a sufficient condition for a "creative response."

The common structure of the Pakistani, Peruvian, and Uruguayan projects can now be formulated as follows:

1. If the project planners (and this usually includes the World Bank officials involved in financing the project) had known in advance all the difficulties and troubles that were lying in store for the project, they probably would never have touched it, because a gloomy view would have been taken of the country's ability to overcome these difficulties by calling into play political, administrative, or technical creativity.

2. In some, though not all, of these cases advance knowledge of these difficulties would therefore have been unfortunate, for the difficulties and the ensuing search for solutions

set in motion a train of events that not only rescued the project but often made it particularly valuable.

WE MAY BE DEALING HERE with a general principle of action: Creativity always comes as a surprise to us; therefore we can never count on it and we dare not believe in it until it has happened. In other words, we would not consciously engage upon tasks whose success clearly requires that creativity be forthcoming. Hence, the only way in which we can bring our creative resources fully into play is by misjudging the nature of the task, by presenting it to ourselves as more routine, simple, undemanding of genuine creativity than it will turn out to be.

Or, put differently: since we necessarily underestimate our creativity, it is desirable that we underestimate to a roughly similar extent the difficulties of the tasks we face so as to be tricked by these two offsetting underestimates into undertaking tasks that we can, but otherwise would not dare, tackle. The principle is important enough to deserve a name: since we are apparently on the trail here of some sort of invisible or hidden hand that beneficially hides difficulties from us, I propose the Hiding Hand.

Before relegating the Hiding Hand to the developing countries as its special realm, we shall briefly elaborate the statement that we may be dealing here with a fairly general phenomenon that permits us to understand or reinterpret certain aspects of human behavior and history. The principle suggests that, far from seeking out and taking up challenges, people typically take on and plunge into new tasks because of the erroneously presumed absence of a challenge, because the task looks easier and more manageable than it will turn out to be.

What we are trying to say can be well conveyed by taking Marx's famous sentence: "Mankind always takes up only such problems as it can solve," and by modifying its wording slightly, but its meaning fundamentally, to read: "Mankind always takes up only such problems as *it thinks* it can solve." Addition of the italicized words thoroughly blurs the neat determinacy of Marx's original statement; for, with this version, it is possible that, as a result of various misconceptions about its problem-solving ability, "mankind" will take up either more or fewer problems than it actually can solve at the moment it takes them up. Up to a point, the Hiding Hand can help accelerate the rate at which "mankind" engages successfully in problem-solving: it takes up problems *it thinks* it can solve, finds they are really more difficult than expected, but then, being stuck with them, attacks willy-nilly the unsuspected difficulties—and sometimes even succeeds.

Looking backward on this kind of sequence, an interpretation in terms of some challenge-and-response mechanism seems to be quite consistent with the facts and, of course, it is much more flattering to our ego. Indeed, people who have stumbled through the experience just described will tend to retell it as though they had known the difficulties all along and had bravely gone to meet them—*fare bella figura* is a strong human propensity.[2] While we are rather willing and even eager and relieved to agree with a historian's finding that we stumbled into the more shameful events of history such as war, we are correspondingly unwilling to concede—in fact we find it intolerable to imagine—that our more lofty achievements, such as economic, social, or political progress, could have come about by stumbling rather than through careful planning, rational behavior, and the courageous taking up of a

2. Exceptions to this behavior are provided by exceptional men such as Luther who, upon looking back on his life, acknowledged the role of the Hiding Hand most explicitly: "Had I known all in advance, God would have been put to great trouble to bring me to it. . . . God has led me on as if I were a horse and he put blinkers on me so that I could not see who came running up upon me." Quoted from the *Tischreden* in Wilhelm Pauck, *The Heritage of the Reformation* (rev. ed.; Free Press, 1961), pp. 20–21. This passage was shown to me by Lisa Hirschman.

clearly perceived challenge. Language itself conspires toward this sort of asymmetry: man falls into error, but not into truth.

WHILE SOME PRESENCE of the Hiding Hand may be helpful or required in eliciting action under all latitudes, it is no doubt specially needed where the tradition of problem-solving is weak and where invention and innovation have not yet been institutionalized or routinized. In other words, in developed countries less hiding of the uncertainties and likely difficulties of a prospective task is required than in underdeveloped countries where confidence in creativity is lacking. In the former there are large numbers of achievement-motivated actors who have acquired "the conviction that [they] can modify the outcome of an uncertain situation by [their] own personal achievements";[3] in the latter, on the contrary, new tasks harboring many unknowns must often be presented as though they were all "cut and dried" in order to be undertaken. Hopefully, the experience that difficulties can be successfully handled will eventually permit a more candid appraisal of tasks and projects.

The Hiding Hand principle has several fairly close relatives. The idea that failure fully to *visualize* prospective *internal* costs can be growth-promoting is, in a sense, an extension of the more familiar and more obvious thought that disregard of the costs a new project or industry will inflict on third parties —that is, failure to *internalize external* costs—can serve as a stimulus to enterprise.[4] In both cases, total costs are underestimated and investment decisions activated in consequence.

3. David C. McClelland, *The Achieving Society* (Van Nostrand, 1961), p. 224.
4. I discussed this possibility at some length in *The Strategy of Economic Development* (Yale University Press, 1958), pp. 57–61. Failure to internalize external costs is probably most typical of new ventures in product-substituting (rather than product-adding) industries, while the failure fully to visualize internal costs affects the various categories of public and private investment decisions in quite a different pattern. See below, pp. 17–21.

There is, however, an important difference: When internal costs or difficulties are inadequately visualized, the project or firm will find itself in financial trouble unless an offset to these costs is encountered. When external costs are disregarded, on the other hand, the venture can yield a private profit without further ado. Nevertheless, the external costs too require an offset if the venture is to be judged a success from society's point of view.[5]

An even closer approximation to the Hiding Hand principle was formulated several years ago by an economic historian, John Sawyer. Having looked at development projects that were undertaken in the first half of the nineteenth century in the United States, he noted that underestimates of cost resulting from "miscalculation or sheer ignorance" were, in a number of great and ultimately successful economic undertakings—particularly in transport and in the opening up of new resources— "crucial to getting an enterprise launched at all." "Had the total investment required been accurately and objectively known at the beginning, the project would not have been begun." The eventual success of these ventures, in spite of the large initial miscalculation and the consequent financial trouble at various stages, derived from the fact that, once the necessary funds were secured and the project was brought to completion, "the error in estimating costs was at least offset by a corresponding error in the estimation of demand."[6]

The resemblance between this idea and the Hiding Hand principle is obvious. There is a double underestimate of both costs and benefits in Sawyer's scheme, while we have observed similarly, if more broadly, a double underestimate of the variout difficulties that lie across the project's path, on the one

5. For the nature of this offset, see *ibid.*, p. 61.
6. John E. Sawyer, "Entrepreneurial Error and Economic Growth," *Explorations in Entrepreneurial History*, Vol. 4 (May 1952), pp. 199, 200.

hand, and of the ability to solve these difficulties, on the other. The difference is that Sawyer's model is focused primarily on the underestimate of costs which is presented as being due to the entrepreneur's activity drive and optimism combined with the knowledge that there is a ceiling to the amount that can be raised for the project. The underestimate of benefits is unexplained and acts rather as a *deus ex machina* to save selected projects that turn out to cost much more than expected.

In our Hiding Hand principle, Sawyer's unexplained underestimate of benefits becomes the underestimate, on the part of the project planner, of his own problem-solving ability and, as we have seen, this underestimate has a satisfactory rationale. The principle then goes on to state that in view of this underestimate an offsetting underestimate of the difficulties themselves is required so that perfectly feasible and potentially productive projects will actually be undertaken. We shall now explore in more detail the circumstances under which the Hiding Hand is likely to come into play. Which are the projects, in other words, that tend to be undertaken because their difficulties are liable to be underestimated? And which ones tend to be systematically neglected because their difficulties are too obvious? These questions make it evident that the Hiding Hand, while permitting an increase in the rate at which projects are taken up, also leads to a bias in project selection.

It becomes clear, for example, that projects derive a crucial advantage from being based on a technique that *looks* transferable even though it may not actually be nearly as copiable as it looks. This is perhaps a principal reason that infrastructural and industrial projects have so large an edge over others: not that the techniques involved are in fact so exceedingly transferable, for time and again industrial projects, particularly those that are not limited to administering "last touches" to a host of imported semifinished inputs, run into considerable technical and managerial difficulties when they are transplanted to a different environment. But factories look as though they could be picked up and dropped anywhere, whereas in such activities as agriculture and education the need for adaptation and the concomitant problems are immediately obvious. Industry thus lends itself eminently to the operation of the Hiding Hand, whereas agricultural projects suffer from the abandon and sincerity with which they flaunt their prospective difficulties.[7]

This conclusion is reinforced when the principle of the Hiding Hand is viewed in the perspective of time. For its mechanism to work, it is necessary that the operators be thoroughly "caught" by the time the unsuspected difficulties appear—caught in the sense that having spent considerable money, time, and energy and having committed their prestige, they will be strongly motivated to generate all the problem-solving energy of which they are capable.

Just as the Hiding Hand principle states that the to-be-experienced difficulties should be hidden at the moment of the decision to go ahead with the project, so it *implies* that these difficulties should not appear *too early* after the execution of the project has started, for, at least within a certain range, the propensity to tackle the difficulties will be roughly proportional to the effort, financial and otherwise, already furnished. Therefore, a given level of difficulties may be wholly discouraging for the prosecution of the project if it turns up early, while it would be tackled with alacrity and perhaps solved if it arose at a later stage.

7. In the last section of this chapter, we discuss the exaggeration of benefits as an action-inducing mechanism which is an alternative to the Hiding Hand when a project's prospective difficulties are too obvious to be hidden away. But agricultural projects do not lend themselves too well to the operation of this mechanism either.

In spite of the somewhat paradoxical ring of this assertion—paradoxical only because medical science has impregnated us with the notion that the sooner a malady is recognized and diagnosed the better—it appears to be confirmed by experience with development projects, and it again underlines the disadvantageous position of agricultural as compared with industrial and infrastructural projects. With the (important) exceptions of irrigation and tree-crop projects, agricultural projects have a short gestation period and therefore production or marketing difficulties unfold rather soon after the projects have been started; hence, attempts to rescue them are often half-hearted and they are readily pronounced failures and abandoned. This is the story of many colonization projects in Latin America and Africa.[8]

In projects with longer gestation periods and more permanent structures, similar difficulties tend to appear much later, and far more serious efforts are made to overcome them. This difference between projects with short and long gestation periods is well illustrated by the contrasting fates of the East African Groundnut Scheme and the Owen Falls Hydroelectric Station in Uganda. Undertaken at the same time (in the immediate postwar period), in the same region, by the same kind of colonial administrators wishing to turn over a new progressive leaf and harboring similar illusions about the nature of the development process, both schemes were financially unsuccessful during their early years. The Groundnut Scheme was soon abandoned and hardly anything remains of it; the Owen Falls Station, on the other hand, had many lean years,

8. It is difficult to gain an understanding of the history of these projects, for they leave hardly any trace behind as the once-to-be-colonized lands revert to bush and the project planners and operators to silence. One good case study is in K. D. S. Baldwin, *The Niger Agricultural Project: An Experiment in African Development* (Harvard University Press, 1957).

but it endured and finally came into its own and will soon have to be supplemented by new generating capacity. Once it had become clear that the originally anticipated industrial boom in the Owen Falls area was not going to materialize, the Uganda Electricity Board made an effort to tap new markets for its power, building transmission lines to neighboring Kenya at first and then to a host of smaller industries and towns of Uganda.

By itself, the mere ability of the Owen Falls Station to survive cannot of course be taken as a vindication of the original investment decision. While later administrators were right in considering as bygone the heavy costs that had been sunk into the project in its early years, the project as a whole may still have to be given a poor mark. It is well known that with long-gestation projects one runs the risk that good money will be thrown after bad. We are here pointing out that short-gestation projects are subject to the opposite risk: the failure to throw good money after what looks bad, but could be turned into good, if only the requisite rescue effort were forthcoming. When, as is often the case, the outcome of such an effort is highly uncertain at the time it is undertaken, the probability that the effort will be made increases with the costs that will have been sunk into the project by the time the difficulties appear.[9]

The foregoing remarks permit a policy conclusion: Projects whose potential difficulties and disappointments are apt to

9. This proposition is related to the findings of psychologists that members of a club or group who have paid high initiation fees or gone through severe initiation rites are liable to find the group activities more fascinating than low-fee members. Compare E. Aronson and J. Mills, "The Effects of Severity of Initiation on Liking for a Group," *Journal of Abnormal and Social Psychology,* Vol. 59 (1959), pp. 177–81. In the same spirit, we are suggesting in the text that when there is room for making the group activities more interesting, the required initiative is likely to be forthcoming from the high-fee, rather than from the low-fee, members.

manifest themselves at an early stage should be administered by agencies having a long-term commitment to the success of the projects. They should be developed as much as possible in an experimental spirit, in the style of a pilot project gathering strength and experience gradually, so that they may escape being classed and closed down as failures in their infancy. The Uruguayan livestock and pasture improvement project followed both these precepts and has thus been able to survive and to achieve maturity and success.

PROMOTERS AND DEVELOPERS must long have been dimly aware of the Hiding Hand principle, for they have been remarkably adept at finding ways in which projects that would normally be discriminated against because they are too obviously replete with difficulties and uncertainties can be made to look more attractive to the decision maker.

One widely practiced method consists in pretending that a project is nothing but a straightforward application of a well-known technique that has been used successfully elsewhere. For example, for a number of years after World War II, any river valley development scheme, whether it concerned the São Francisco River in Brazil, the Papaloapan River in Mexico, the Cauca in Colombia, the Dez in Iran, or the Damodar in eastern India, was presented to a reassured public as a true copy—if possible, certified expressly by David Lilienthal—of the Tennessee Valley Authority. Although obviously two river valley development schemes will differ vastly more from one another than two Coca Cola bottling plants, the impression was created, by the appeal to the "TVA model," that clear sailing lay ahead for the proposed schemes. To be acceptable, it seems, a project must often be billed as a pure replica of a successful venture in an advanced country.

It is no doubt a pity that ventures that are 90 percent indigenous initiative and execution and 10 percent imitation of a foreign model are regularly presented to the public as though the percentages were, in fact, reversed, but this seems to be the price that must sometimes be paid to "sell" projects that would otherwise look too forbidding.

This attempt at making a project's path look smoother than it is may be termed the "pseudo-imitation" technique. When the novelty or difficulty of the task is too obvious for this technique to be plausible another method is often used. It consists in dismissing previous efforts at solving the task as "piecemeal" and in pretending to more insight than is actually available by drawing up a "comprehensive program." It can be called the "pseudo-comprehensive-program" technique.[10]

An excellent example of this technique is supplied by the Uruguayan livestock and pasture improvement project. It started with the avowed aim of "implementing" a joint mission report issued in 1951 by the World Bank and the United Nations Food and Agriculture Organization. The report's recommendations covered an extremely wide spectrum, as will appear from the following incomplete list of topics: subdivision of pastures by fences, grazing trials, tree plantings on permanent grasslands, introduction of legumes, increased use of lime and phosphate, shrub eradication, works to control runoff water, establishment of fodder reserves through silage and hay, better storage facilities, changes in the cropping system to include legumes, establishment of diversified farming combining harvested crops and livestock, improvement in productivity by irrigation, tillage practices, weed and pest control, erosion control, control of animal disease, improvement in transportation, storage and marketing, organization of research

10. This technique is a variant of the "pseudo-creative" response which I discussed in *Journeys Toward Progress: Studies of Economic Policy-Making in Latin America* (Twentieth Century Fund, 1963), pp. 239 ff.

and technical services, appropriate price and other economic policies, etc.[11]

Such a report tends to give the policy makers and project planners the illusion that the "experts" have already found all the answers to the problems and that all that is needed is faithful "implementation" of these multifarious recommendations. In fact, Uruguayan agriculture had shown prolonged and stubborn resistance to many of the report's proposals which were by no means new; the reason was that considerable and difficult breakthroughs remained to be achieved in technical, organizational, and other realms. But the comprehensive-program technique underplays this need for imagination, insight, and the application of creative energies, and the project planners are, as it were, tricked into undertaking a program whose real difficulties will only gradually become apparent to them.

The comprehensive program whose many components are given equal emphasis and are pronounced to be interrelated in effect covers up the ignorance of the experts about the real cure of the malady they have been summoned to examine; if they knew, they would be proposing a far more sharply focused program. Incidentally, the diffuse kind of program provides at the same time an excellent alibi to the experts in case anything goes wrong: since it is practically impossible to carry out all the proposed actions, any troubles can be blamed on the failure to follow the experts' instructions rather than on the shortcomings of their advice.

Real interdependencies exist, no doubt, and a multipronged attack on a problem is therefore often necessary. But a comprehensive program that stems from real insight into the problem

11. International Bank for Reconstruction and Development and Food and Agriculture Organization of the United Nations, *The Agricultural Development of Uruguay*, 1951. (Processed.)

will be easy to distinguish from one that is a smoke screen for ignorance, for in the former the nature of the interdependencies will be clearly spelled out and an effort will have been made, in the interests of feasibility, to limit the number of activities that have to be undertaken concurrently.[12] This sort of *minimization of balanced growth requirements* which has all the marks of insight into the problem was evident in a 1964 plan for the creation of an industrial pole in the Taranto-Bari-Brindisi area in southern Italy: a deliberate effort was made to determine a strictly limited number of establishments producing intermediate goods and providing services, such as tool making, that would have to be available if a certain group of newly planned mechanical industries were to find it attractive to locate at the "pole."[13]

Regional development programs supply additional illustrations that certain comprehensive programs function, in effect, as "servants" of the Hiding Hand. Here also the programs traced out in advance must be as comprehensive and multifarious as possible to build up the morale of the slightly frightened decision makers; for, in addition to overcoming their ignorance about the path to progress for their region or valley, they must do battle with various powerful contrary interests and must therefore form as broad a coalition as pos-

12. A recent, very interesting attempt to formulate a theory of design has come to a similar conclusion: the correct method for solving design problems when the ultimate solution has to satisfy numerous interdependent requirements is not to treat the system of requirements as an interdependent whole, but to define "isolable subsystems," that is, subsystems among which there is a minimum amount of interdependence, and then to adjust the resulting partial designs to each other. Christopher Alexander, *Notes on the Synthesis of Form* (Harvard University Press, 1964), pp. 40–43 and *passim*.

13. Italconsult, *Studio per la promozione di un polo industriale di sviluppo in Italia Meridionale* (Rome, 1964), Pt. 2, Chaps. 3–4. (Processed.)

sible by promising something to every important section within the region or valley.

The foregoing is a fairly accurate description of what happened in the case of the development program for Italy's south. The Cassa per il Mezzogiorno was charged with undertaking a vast complex of programs and its activities reached virtually into every nook and cranny of its huge territory. But in the course of undertaking its public works programs, the Cassa soon learned that some were far more efficient and growth-promoting than others. In 1958 a prominent meridionalist, distinguishing between the (unserviceable) "bones" and the (valuable) "meat" of southern agriculture, pointed out that the "meat"—the portion where Cassa investments could be expected to yield high returns—comprised only about half a million hectares of irrigated or irrigable valley lands. Most of the rest of the area where the Cassa had operated—some 11 million hectares—were now dismissed as "bones."[14] The Cassa's proposed concentration of effort on irrigable land became in effect its new agricultural program when the agency's life was extended for a further period of fifteen years in 1965. It was far removed from the all-inclusive approach the Cassa had set out to implement; but just as the managers of Uruguay's livestock program had come to realize that the key to agricultural progress was the introduction of legumes, so the Cassa had found out in fifteen years of "implementation" of its comprehensive program that the larger payoffs of its agricultural program were to be obtained by concentration on the few fertile flat areas that dot the coastal lands of the south.

14. Manlio Rossi-Doria, *Dieci anni di politica agraria nel Mezzogiorno* (Bari, Italy: Laterza, 1958), p. xix. In this, his original formulation of the meat-bones (*polpa-osso*) dichotomy, Rossi-Doria included 1.5 million hectares suitable for highly productive nonirrigable tree crops and vineyards in the "meat." But in later usage, this term became increasingly restricted to irrigable lands.

THE TWO PURVEYORS of the Hiding Hand—the pseudo-imitation technique and the pseudo-comprehensive-program technique—are nicely complementary: the former makes projects appear less difficulty-ridden than they really are, whereas the latter gives the project planners the illusion that they are in possession of far more insight into the projects' difficulties than is as yet available. Both techniques act essentially as crutches for the decision maker, permitting him to go forward at a stage when he has not yet acquired enough confidence in his problem-solving ability to make a more candid appraisal of a project's prospective difficulties and of the risks he is assuming. The experience of meeting with these difficulties and risks and of being able to deal with them should then enable him to discard these crutches and to achieve a more mature appraisal of new projects. The recourse to the Hiding Hand thus becomes less necessary as development proceeds, and one of the indirect benefits of projects is precisely that the willingness of the decision maker to face uncertainty and difficulty is increased. The Hiding Hand is essentially a mechanism *that makes the risk-averter take risks* and in the process turns him into less of a risk-averter. In this manner, it opens an escape from one of those formidable "prerequisites" or "preconditions" to development; it permits the so-called prerequisite to come into existence *after* the event to which it is supposed to be the prerequisite. In our model, risk-taking behavior is engaged in actively (though involuntarily) prior to the arrival on the stage of the "risk-taking, achievement-motivated personality"; instead, it is this personality that is fashioned by risk-taking behavior.[15]

15. For a general argument about this sort of inverted sequence, and an appeal to the theory of cognitive dissonance for explaining it, see my article, "Obstacles to Development: A Classification and a Quasi-Vanishing Act," *Economic Development and Cultural Change*, Vol. 13 (July 1965), pp. 385–93.

The Hiding Hand model is helpful in understanding the process of growth from yet another point of view. It has often been remarked that what is most needed at an early stage in development is unqualified success for the ventures that are undertaken so that the spirit of entrepreneurship may become strong and widely spread. But this prescription is singularly unhelpful since in the early stages of any development effort numerous disappointments are inevitable, and mere survival is a feat for the innovator. How is development possible then? Perhaps because among many of the ventures that do survive, the Hiding Hand has been at work: in them, the entrepreneurs' experience will have been neither wholly better nor entirely worse than expected, but in a sense *both worse* (getting into unsuspected trouble) and *better* (getting unexpectedly out of it); and even though their financial success is not striking, the resulting infusion of confidence, and perhaps the discovery of a more "exciting" way of life, will strengthen the spirit of enterprise.

In effect, then, the contribution of development ventures depends not only on their—properly discounted—financial returns, but on important side effects which will often be reflected in the time shape of these returns. Specifically, when a venture has gone through considerable teething trouble as a result of the intervention of the Hiding Hand, it is likely to deserve a higher ranking than one with a similar return but no such experience.

We have ended up here with an economic argument strikingly paralleling Christianity's oft expressed preference for the repentant sinner over the righteous man who never strays from the path of virtue. And essentially the same idea, even though formulated, as one might expect, in a vastly different spirit, is found in Nietzsche's maxim "That which does not destroy me, makes me stronger." This sentence admirably epitomizes several of our project histories.

HAVING ACHIEVED, in a roundabout way, a convergence of
benefit-cost analysis with the teachings of philosophy and re-
ligion, I should probably stop right here. Unfortunately, however, this dramatic effect must be spoiled; for something must
be said about the dangers and failures of the Hiding Hand.
As noted before, its principal usefulness is in inducing risk-
averters to commit themselves to risk-taking behavior. This
commitment permits an acceleration of economic growth; as
a result of their experiences, decision makers are likely to become readier to look newly emerging risk-laden situations
straight in the face. The Hiding Hand is thus essentially a
transition mechanism through which decision makers learn to
take risks, and *the shorter the transition and the faster the
learning the better.* For this mode of learning about risk is not
without grave dangers. One has to be rather lucky to be lured
by the Hiding Hand into ventures whose emergent problems
and difficulties can be successfully tackled. As long as one
needs this "crutch" in order to act, the probability of com-
mitting major errors and of undertaking projects that will turn
into failures is obviously higher than when he is able to differ-
entiate between acceptable and nonacceptable risk.

Moreover, those servants of the Hiding Hand—the pseudo-
imitation and the pseudo-comprehensive-program techniques
—have hardly been described in flattering terms. One reason
is precisely that while these techniques facilitate decision
making, they can easily be habit-forming rather than self-
liquidating. The camouflage they use to disguise pioneering
entrepreneurship may go undetected for a long time and may
continue to be used when it is no longer needed. Moreover,
these techniques have a number of undesirable side effects.
The pseudo-imitation technique will not permit a country to
reap the full psychological benefit of the ventures successfully
launched under its auspices since there will remain a lingering
feeling that any achievement is due to the imitation of a for-

eign model. The pseudo-comprehensive-program technique may, even after a favorable outcome, leave a sense of disappointment and frustration; for, if our description of the process by which insight into the problem is finally achieved is correct, then a number of originally enunciated measures and objectives that were important elements in the "comprehensive program" will no longer be actively pursued once the most promising approach is discovered. As a result, public opinion will tend to lament the abandonment of originally much touted programs and the project, even though a success, will leave behind a vague sense of failure. This is exactly what happened when the Cassa decided to pick the "meat" from the "bones" and when the Damodar Valley Corporation concentrated its work more and more on power generation.

BEFORE CONCLUDING it may be of interest to place the phenomenon here described in a wider context. The Hiding Hand is essentially a way of inducing action through error, the error being an underestimate of the project's costs or difficulties. As Sawyer noted for his related theory of entrepreneurial error, the argument smacks uncomfortably of "praise of folly"—a praise that is sometimes deserved but always needs to be narrowly circumscribed.

We bestowed limited praise on the Hiding Hand because, by hiding prospective difficulties and by thus inducing an underestimate of costs, it serves to offset another error that project planners are liable to commit through their propensity to underrate their own inventiveness and problem-solving ability; when this propensity is present, the chances for correct project decisions to be taken will actually improve, up to a point, as the Hiding Hand does its handiwork. Suppose, however, that prospective difficulties stand clearly revealed and that the actors are afflicted by the same lack of self-confidence; the prospective costs will now tend to be overestimated, and the only remaining way by which action on perfectly feasible projects can still be induced is through a corresponding over-estimate of the prospective benefits—we need a magnifying glass for benefits, to take the place of the mechanism that hid the difficulties and shrunk the costs. Thus, the same basic infirmity, namely lack of confidence in one's ability to overcome difficulties, requires correction either by understating the difficulties or by compensating the exaggerated image they project by a similar exaggeration of the project's expected accomplishments.

Exaggeration of prospective benefits is at least as common a device to elicit action as underestimation of costs. This error, specially when it is combined with an underestimate of costs, has of course often led to disaster—history abounds with examples, from bankruptcies and white elephants to lost or ruinously won wars. But just as the hiding of costs, the exaggeration of benefits can occasionally serve to ward off another, less visible, but nonetheless real, disaster: missed opportunity.

This is the case when difficulties in the project's path are unhideable. Take, for example, projects that clearly require from the start the making of politically difficult decisions such as a change in existing administrative structures around which considerable vested interests have gathered. This was the case of the Damodar Valley Corporation whose basic charter meant surrender of important powers of the states of West Bengal and Bihar (and to some extent also of the central government) to the new agency. To justify so unprecedented a move, it became necessary for the promoters of the agency to make such extravagant claims as that it would transform the Damodar Valley into "India's Ruhr" or that it would promote rapid, harmonious, and integrated development of all of the valley's natural and human resources, when in effect its task was rather narrowly limited to flood control, electric power generation, and some irrigation.

Extravagance in promising future benefits can thus often be found and may play a useful role in those development projects that require difficult initial decisions, be it a change in existing institutions or a fiscal sacrifice demanded of some or all of the citizenry. Actually the promise of some sort of utopia is most characteristic of larger-scale undertakings such as the launching of social reforms or of external aggression because they are likely to require heavy initial sacrifices.

Recourse to the utopian vision as a stimulant to action has on occasion been advocated in a sweeping way. The Hiding Hand or, in its absence, the exaggeration of benefits has been considered useful as a means of dealing with a specific and temporary infirmity of some societies, that is, man's inadequate acquaintance with his ability to solve difficulties. A far more generalized pessimism about human nature as weak-willed, routine-ridden, and decadence-prone led Georges Sorel to the belief that humanity required "myths"—inspiring images of battle and triumph—for any substantial forward movement. He was so well aware of the disproportion between the promises of these myths and the ensuing reality that he simply vetoed what is today called project reappraisal: "We should be especially careful," he said, "not to make any comparison between accomplished fact and the picture people had formed for themselves before action."[16] It is strange that Sorel did not realize how unlikely it was that his injunction against looking back would be heeded any more than that of Hades to Orpheus.

A far more appealing and convincing defense of the occasional need for exaggeration of prospective benefits appears in an essay by Kolakowski, the Polish philosopher:

16. *Reflections on Violence*, trans. T. E. Hulme (Peter Smith, 1941), p. 22.

The simplest improvements in social conditions require so huge an effort on the part of society that full awareness of this disproportion would be most discouraging and would thereby make any social progress impossible. The effort must be prodigally great if the result is to be at all visible. . . . It is not at all peculiar then that this terrible disproportion must be quite weakly reflected in human consciousness if society is to generate the energy required to effect changes in social and human relations. For this purpose, one exaggerates the prospective results into a myth so as to make them take on dimensions which correspond a bit more to the immediately felt effort. . . . [The myth acts like] a Fata Morgana which makes beautiful lands arise before the eyes of the members of a caravan and thus increases their efforts to the point where, in spite of all their sufferings, they reach the next tiny waterhole. Had such tempting mirages not appeared, the exhausted caravan would inevitably have perished in the sandstorm, bereft of hope.[17]

This fine passage permits two observations. First of all, in contrast to what must have been Sorel's assumption when he issued his injunction against looking back, the Kolakowski image definitely conveys the message that the effort of the caravan was worth the cost and the suffering since it permitted survival. Secondly, the effort would not have been forthcoming had there not been the Fata Morgana, that is, a rather serious overestimate of the benefits.

The similarity to the justification for the Hiding Hand is striking. In Kolakowski's thought (which is of course concerned with large-scale sociopolitical movements and action rather than with development projects) the exaggeration of benefits is required for precisely the reason indicated earlier: the actors underestimate the strength that is left in them; therefore the to-be-furnished effort is felt as "impossible" until the required social energy is generated by the mirage.

17. Leszek Kolakowski, *Der Mensch ohne Alternative* (Munich: R. Piper, 1961), pp. 127–28. My translation from the German translation.

The Fata Morgana image contains one other suggestion, rather different from the use Kolakowski makes of it: there may be special difficulties in visualizing in advance *intermediate* outcomes or *partial* successes such as the "tiny waterhole." In other words, the utopian vision may be necessary not so much to offset the inflated costs of the proposed enterprise as to compensate for an infirmity of man's imagination; for even though costs may not appear unduly high, man may simply be unable to conceive of the strictly limited, yet satisfactory, advances, replete with compromises and concessions to opposing forces, which are the very stuff of "incremental politics"[18] as well as the frequent result of ambitious socioeconomic development moves. The Damodar Valley story furnishes a good illustration for this kind of development: from the early fifties on, the Damodar Valley Corporation was increasingly hemmed in by encroachments on its original powers by the states of West Bengal and Bihar, and little remained in the mid-1960's of the majestic vision of integrated development of the valley's resources under the agency's unified command; yet the contribution of the agency's installations to industrial, urban, and resource development has fully justified the major portion of the investments the agency undertook, and it is doubtful that these investments would have been made without the stimulus of the initial vision.

We have now identified two situations in which overestimates of benefits can play a positive role: (1) when, because of inexperience in problem-solving, the actors have an exaggerated idea of the costs and difficulties of action, and (2) when, because of inexperience with the actual processes of change, the actors are unable to visualize intermediate outcomes and limited advances. As in the case of the Hiding Hand with its

18. David Braybrooke and C. E. Lindblom, *A Strategy of Decision* (Free Press, 1963), pp. 71–77.

underestimate of costs and difficulties, and pending the correction of these various inexperiences, the overestimate of benefits must therefore be recognized as a useful development mechanism for a transitional phase.

But, for the reasons already given, it is much to be desired that this transitional phase be short. The very description-exposé of these mechanisms of self-deception that has been attempted here may persuade project planners to dispense with these crutches as soon as it is possible for them to do so.

A more effective cure could come with improved knowledge of various aspects of project behavior. To acquire elements of such knowledge is the purpose of the next chapters.

CHAPTER TWO

Uncertainties

THE HIDING HAND does its work essentially through ignorance of ignorance, of uncertainties, and of difficulties. Therefore, if we wish to avoid immoderate use of it in making project decisions, our first task is to become aware in some detail of the uncertainties that affect projects and of the resulting difficulties they may have to encounter and overcome.

The incidence of the unknown, the uncertain, and the hazardous differs vastly from one kind of project to another. The term "project" conjures up the notion of a set of blueprints, prepared by consulting engineers, which, upon being handed to a contractor, will be transformed into three-dimensional reality within a reasonable time period. Some types of projects come fairly close to this concept; others, however, are of a completely different nature and are poorly described by the word "project" which implies far more certainty and knowledge than is available.

Similarly, the term "implementation" understates the complexity of the task of carrying out projects that are affected by a high degree of initial ignorance and uncertainty. Here "project implementation" may often mean in fact a long voyage of discovery in the most varied domains, from technology to politics.

In this chapter we shall first review the various ways in which projects can run into trouble and then attempt to understand the differential propensities of different kinds of projects to run into these various troubles. In using the term "uncertainty" to designate this propensity toward difficulty, we may seem to be stretching its technical meaning, and we must insert a brief note to justify our usage.

It will of course be admitted that uncertainty could be closely associated with the propensity of a project toward difficulty. When information about the likelihood of a possible future difficulty or of a corresponding "lucky break" is simply not available, we would probably consider the project as reasonably difficulty-prone, and uncertainty would be the reason for this judgment. But what about the perhaps more common case in which, quite simply, the probability of the project's encounter with difficulty is high and is known to be high? To consider such a situation as replete with uncertainty seems highly questionable. Our justification for doing so lies in the fact that the encounter with difficulty is only the first step in a two-step sequence: the second step is the wrestling with difficulty which produces a whole range of possible outcomes, from victoriously overcoming the difficulty to wholly succumbing to it. In other words, even if there were complete certainty about the encounter with difficulty, there would remain considerable uncertainty about the final outcome.

One further consideration is in order. If the difficulty is encountered and overcome, the benefits that accrue as a result are likely to be the higher, the greater were the odds against a favorable outcome. This sort of association between risk and payoff is standard in "fair" games of chance. In real-life situations, however, risks frequently increase without any corresponding increase in the payoff: for example, the risk that a plane will crash becomes larger as it runs into a storm, yet there is no concomitant increase in the benefits the passengers receive in case they arrive safely. But in the situations I shall describe, the payoff does increase: a high probability that the project will fall on hard times as a result of the technological or administrative or demand problems it may experience has, as a rule, a counterpart in the correspondingly high payoffs that accrue in various forms if these problems are solved.[1] In terms of characteristics of a function assigning a probability to each possible outcome, a high propensity for a project to run into trouble means therefore not a smaller expected value than would result from a low propensity, but a higher variance; that is, precisely, a higher degree of uncertainty. Herein lies an additional justification for our terminology.

Varieties of Uncertainties

The numerous uncertainties affecting projects fall naturally into two familiar and fundamental categories: those connected with the production of the intended output of the project—the supply side—and those connected with the demand for the output. All problems arising during construction belong to the supply side, whereas problems arising during operation can originate in either the supply or the demand side. Within the supply and demand classification there are the following kinds of uncertainties:

1. On the supply side of the project, we first have the technology of the project itself: uncertainty may surround the process by which outputs are to be produced from inputs, as well as the availability of the required material inputs at approximately the anticipated prices.

2. Next, uncertainty on the supply side may center around the human factor. This very general category includes the possibility that, in construction as well as operation, the project may experience problems of labor supply, of staffing in gen-

1. For example, learning, confidence, etc., but often also more tangible matters, such as the diversification of the raw material base for the Karna-phuli Paper Mill, which was an indirect result of the difficulty—bamboo flowering—encountered by the mill.

eral, and of intergroup relations; problems of management, in particular with regard to the efficiency and viability of perhaps novel administrative arrangements; or problems deriving from outside political interference with the project's affairs.

3. Finally, on the supply side, one has to contend with financial uncertainty about completion of the project. This uncertainty, seemingly very important, will be considered only briefly because it is largely conditioned by technological and administrative uncertainties.

4. Uncertainty on the demand side has perhaps received widest attention because of the well-recognized danger of a project becoming a "white elephant" as a result of inadequate demand for its outputs. Actually, because of input-output relations, it is sometimes a rather arbitrary matter to decide whether a problem has arisen on the demand or the supply side. Some projects are not considered complete until they have delivered a final product to the consumer, while others have a less ambitious mission. As a result, what appears as a demand problem in the latter projects shows up as a technological difficulty in the former. For example, when an electric power station has large unutilized capacity, this is identified as a demand problem; but when irrigation waters are not used for growing crops, we tend to say that the project has failed to solve its supply task since by convention its output is not just water, but the additional farm products anticipated as farmers utilize the irrigation facilities. Though arbitrary and conventional, these delimitations of a project's task are significant, as will be seen, in prescribing remedies for projects in difficulty.

5. Although demand uncertainties almost automatically focus on the problems of idle capacity, in some types of projects, the opposite risk—namely excess demand—deserves to be taken seriously. As will be seen, it can cause serious group conflict which in turn may threaten the integrity and success of the project.

After having dealt with these uncertainties one by one, we shall point out some interrelations among them and examine to what extent they can—or should—be mitigated.

Supply Uncertainties: Technology

One outstanding case of a project encountering and coming to grips with substantial technological problems, that of the Karnaphuli Paper Mill, has already been told in part. The flowering of the bamboo and the consequent need to find another raw material base for the mill was the principal technological hazard the mill had to face, but it was by no means the only one. At its start, the mill encountered considerable difficulties in operating its chipping, pulping, and particularly its chemical-recovery plants because the silica content of the bamboo was unexpectedly high. This difficulty was traced both to the intrinsic chemical composition of the bamboo species used and to the sand that seeped into the bamboos during the long trip downstream from the stands to the mill. During the first years of operation, some redesigning of the mill became necessary to deal with this problem—in particular, additional washing operations had to be introduced, not only before, but after chipping.

The pasture improvement project in Uruguay is another excellent illustration of what we have called earlier a voyage of discovery. In Chapter 1 we commented on the "pseudo-comprehensive" report issued in 1951 by the World Bank and the Food and Agriculture Organization and on its multifarious recommendations. Except for some valuable experiments by a few progressive and wealthy landowners, nothing much happened in Uruguay's stagnant livestock economy until 1960, when long drawn-out negotiations between the Bank and the Uruguayan government finally resulted in a $7 million loan, to be administered by a newly established Honorary Livestock Commission. The project agreed upon was to involve some

600 medium-sized ranches and was therefore essentially a pilot program that had now been brought down to four principal measures: pasture improvement, subdivisional fencing and provision of additional waterholes, fodder conservation for periods of drought, and disease control. However, the active work of the commission and its experts—technical advisors from New Zealand and Australia played key roles in the program—centered almost wholly on pasture improvement for two good reasons: (1) progress in this area clearly conditions advances in subdivision and in fodder conservation, and probably also in disease control;[2] (2) while the general principles of natural grassland improvement were well known, there remained great areas of technological ignorance about the precise manner of applying those principles in Uruguay.

It may be helpful to show schematically what was known and what remained to be discovered:

Known	*To Be Discovered*
The improvement of permanent grassland depends on an adequate supply of nitrogen, of which the cheapest source is legumes.	Which species of legumes and mixture of legumes and grasses are best suited to the various soils in Uruguay.
Legumes are more easily established in new soil if the seed is inoculated with certain strains of rhizobia, the nitrogen-fixing mechanism.	That noninoculation results in nearly total failure to establish legumes in Uruguay. Which inoculants are efficient under Uruguayan conditions and how the seed is to be inoculated with them.
Satisfactory legume growth depends on an adequate supply of phosphatic fertilizer.	How best to introduce the inoculated legume seed and fertilizer into the natural grasslands.

2. Because more ample and better balanced feed would reduce the incidence of disease, and because more active livestock management conse-

It is clear from the right-hand column that considerable scientific and practical knowledge remained to be acquired before the program could be launched on a big scale. Largely for this reason, disbursements under the loan were quite slow during the first years. But by 1964, information about appropriate varieties of clover, other legumes, grasses, and inoculants was much improved, and the inoculants were being produced in increasing quantity in Uruguay. Also, various methods of implanting the legume seed and fertilizer had been tried out in the participating ranches: instead of the conventional, but excessively slow and expensive, ploughing up of whole fields which were then fertilized and sown to a mixture of grasses and legumes, the commission experimented with and sponsored the introduction of legumes and fertilizer directly into the natural grasslands, first by means of a special machine, the Australian sodseeder, and later by dropping pellets of seeds and fertilizer from airplanes. These methods, which had never been tried in Uruguay, had differential success in different areas, so that by 1964 the commission knew more or less which method should be primarily relied on in the different regions of the country. As a result it was decided that the pilot phase of the project could be concluded and that the program should now be applied over a much wider area. In 1965 the World Bank granted a new loan of $12.7 million for the next phase.

The Uruguayan and Pakistani projects suggest a simple hypothesis on the kind of projects whose course is likely to be particularly marked by technological uncertainty and ignorance: both are closely enmeshed with the natural resources of their respective countries, and the voyage of discovery consists in the acquisition of detailed knowledge of these resources and in the needed adaptation of general scientific and engineering knowledge to them.

---

quent upon subdivision and frequent rotation facilitates disease detection and control.

For this reason, projects that touch a country's terrain only lightly or whose processes require few local material inputs are particularly transferable and "copiable" and therefore free from technological uncertainty: this appears in "infrastructural" projects like telecommunications, electric power transmission, and airlines as well as in the typical "last stage" industries with which the industrialization process based on import substitution has tended to get underway in newly developing countries. As long as standard imported inputs are merely being converted by imported machinery, uncertainty is at a minimum, but it increases as industrialization spreads through backward linkage and as more and more domestic inputs and raw materials are used. Fascinated as economists have been with the desirability of modifying capital-intensive Western technology because of the lower cost of labor in relation to capital typical of the less developed areas, they have failed to notice the considerable modification of standard technology that was often already compelled by specific quality and supply characteristics of various inputs. Conversely, the pressing need to find out how the desired outputs could be produced at all from the local inputs may help to explain why so little effort has been devoted by engineers and industrial managers in developing countries to adapting technology in the labor-intensive direction—they have their hands full with a more crucial task.

Agriculture is of course the economic activity most closely "enmeshed with nature," and agricultural projects are therefore as a rule clearly marked by technological uncertainty—so clearly and almost ostentatiously in fact that, as was pointed out in Chapter 1, developers often shy away from them. Outside of the Uruguayan livestock project, the agricultural projects in our sample all involved irrigation works whose construction usually went smoothly enough, but whose operation was invariably marked by considerable difficulties in utilizing the newly available waters. In part, the reason for these difficulties is precisely the kind of technological uncertainty that marked the Uruguayan project. Except where, as in our Indian or Thai projects, irrigation was meant primarily to supplement rainfall or river overflow and therefore to act essentially as drought insurance, a great deal of new knowledge had to be acquired about the crops that would do well on newly irrigated lands. In some of the southern Italian projects, for example, where irrigation had been expected to lead to livestock fattening and dairying, a number of important innovations surprisingly brought instead the intensive cultivation under irrigation of traditionally dry crops, such as olives and table grapes.

Most of the difficulties experienced by irrigation projects derived, however, not so much from technological ignorance as from the fact that such projects are "systems" whose various components are difficult to fit into place at the same time: besides the construction of the irrigation works, land has to be distributed and settled, new crops have to be grown and new markets found. As a result, irrigation projects partake at the same time of practically every one of our supply and demand uncertainties.

At this point, it appears that uncertainty about a project's ability to supply the desired output at more or less the appointed time is not solely dependent on the degree to which it is enmeshed with the country's natural resources. Another determinant of this uncertainty is likely to be the "system-quality" of the project, that is, the extent to which many interdependent components have to be fitted together and adjusted to each other for the project as a whole to become available and to yield the output for which it was designed. It is preferable to speak of "system-quality" rather than of size; almost invariably large projects will be systems in some sense, but the crucial characteristic that makes for difficulty is not size itself but the need for coordinating and fitting a number of parts into a whole. A 500-mile road could be built mile after mile, starting from one end; in practice, the job is likely to be split into several segments which will be built simultaneously, with separate contracts for the major bridges; as a result there arises the need for coordination and timing of these sub-projects, converting even a "linear" road construction job into something of a system.

Fortunately, many projects are systems to a much smaller extent than they claim at the outset: multiple-purpose river valley development schemes like the one originally sponsored by the Damodar Valley Corporation could function perfectly well with only flood control and electric power generation in place, while the irrigation and navigation components remained uncompleted or nonexistent; similarly the "integrated" Karnaphuli Paper Mill functioned for a while in a most unintegrated fashion, without either local raw material base or chemical-recovery plant. In appraising the system-quality of projects, one must therefore attempt to ascertain the components whose presence and coordination are indispensably required for the project to function.[3]

The following description of the uncertainties of dam construction brings together nicely our two basic uncertainty-causing factors, involvement with local inputs and system-quality:

Dam building is, like commanding a military offensive, an exercise in fitting parts into a whole. It is much less predictable than it sounds. The parts that have to be assembled—reinforcing steel, girders, sluice gates, even stone and above all earth—are not, as you would suppose, uniform and standard. The means by which the assembly is done—the shovels, dumpers, compressors, air hoses, hoists, mixing plants, and especially the men and women—

_____

3. For further comments on this matter, see below, pp. 78–81.

have their own vagaries. The dam building engineer has to be able at once to readjust the combination, to improvise a substitute for the failure, to get the process going again. And, entirely aside from that, there is the river itself, never an entirely known quantity, which may exceed all previous flood heights just when he gets his coffer-dam in place.[4]

Up to now in our discussion, technological uncertainty has been understood as surrounding the processes and methods by which a known product (e.g. paper) is to be produced. Uncertainty can, however, affect also the product itself. It might be objected that it is wrong to use the term "project" for a venture whose intended output is not unequivocally determined. But the fact is that there are many projects with exceedingly vague outputs, such as the development of a river valley or of an economic sector (livestock). Such projects invariably imply voyages of discovery that consist here in focusing gradually on one or several subprojects that can and must be undertaken either because they are truly strategic to the rest of the task, or because it is found that they are the only worthwhile tasks to undertake, or because they are the only ones the project agency is allowed to tackle in view of conflicts with other agencies. That the very broad and all-inclusive initial formulation of sectoral and regional development projects often reflects a high degree of ignorance and uncertainty has already been shown in Chapter 1.

Supply Uncertainties: Administration

It would be impossible to present, within the framework of the present essay, a comprehensive study of "administrative behavior" of projects. But in view of the important role administrative difficulties have played in many of our project his-

4. Henry C. Hart, *Administrative Aspects of River Valley Development* (Asia Publishing House, 1961), p. 16.

tories, an attempt must be made to account for the most important situations in which they occur. While these difficulties —unstable or incompetent management, outside interference, debilitating conflicts, etc.—are closely related to basic social and political factors, the extent to which projects are exposed to them will be seen to vary considerably, within the same sociopolitical setting, from one kind of project to another.

In the first place, projects may experience administrative difficulties because intergroup conflict has been built right into them. Here is a simple formula for doing just that: (1) take a country with deep regional, ethnic, or religious rifts, and (2) place into it a large-scale, nationwide project whose successful operation requires harmony and disciplined cooperation among a staff and labor force which is, or for reasons of interregional equity should be, drawn from all sections of the country.

The Nigerian Railway Corporation fits this formula extremely well. In fact, it has had the worst of both worlds: since it did indeed recruit in all parts of the country, it has been plagued by considerable intergroup friction which became particularly serious in the post-independence period when one group came to occupy all the top management positions; and since recruitment had in effect been far from equally successful in the different regions of the country, the corporation was accused of discriminating in favor of southerners (Ibos in particular) and, in reprisal, was discriminated against in the north whenever there was a choice between giving a load either to a northern trucking firm or to the "Ibo railway."

It is to be noted (see Chapter 4 for more detailed discussion) that operation of the competing mode, that is, highways, does not contain the same source of administrative difficulty: the motor vehicles utilizing them form a multitude of small, independent firms each of which is free and likely to select its personnel in such a way as to minimize intergroup friction.

This very problem of running large-scale or nationwide organizations in countries that are "plural" or "poly-communal" societies[5] should in principle have affected also Uganda's electric power agency and Ethiopia's telecommunications system. While elements of such difficulties were certainly present, they were rather muted and, in fact, one felt or hoped that these organizations might act as training centers for coexistence and cooperation among different ethnic groups. It seems plausible to consider two factors as responsible for this difference: first, the personnel required by electric power and telecommunications is quite small in comparison to railroads so that "clique formation" is more difficult; secondly, apart from the bill-collecting end of the business, both services require largely operation and maintenance of highly complex equipment so that the feeling of belonging to the same technical elite corps may here counteract ethnic antagonism.

Projects that contain the seeds of performance-endangering intergroup conflict can also take shape under conditions somewhat different from those stipulated in the above "formula." Pakistan's Karnaphuli Paper Mill which, while large, was a strictly local venture provides a tragic illustration. In addition to its technological difficulties, the mill experienced during its early years labor troubles largely based on antagonistic feelings between the Bengali labor force and the management team that was preponderantly recruited from non-Bengali Muslims in India and West Pakistan. These troubles erupted in 1955 in riots during which the first general manager of the mill, who had also been its guiding promoter and organizer, was assassi-

5. The term "plural society," which was used by J. S. Furnivall in *Colonial Policy and Practice* (Cambridge University Press, 1948), is contrasted with Western class society by W. A. Lewis in his recent *Politics in West Africa* (Oxford University Press, 1965). The term "poly-communal society" is advocated by F. W. Riggs, *Administration in Developing Countries* (Houghton Mifflin, 1964).

nated. It was then decided that, for some time, expatriate management would be more acceptable to local sensitivities than Pakistani management that was non-Bengali. Here, then, we did not have a nationwide organization, but a complex industrial plant, established in a backward area, whose skill requirements made it necessary to recruit nonindigenous technical personnel. The tragic point of the story is not alone the death of the mill's manager, but the bitter irony of his fate: the mill had been established with the intent of improving and cementing relations between East and West Pakistan by dealing out to the poorer and more populous East one of the new nation's largest industrial ventures.

A second type of problems and conflicts arises when projects disturb, by design or inadvertently, the political, social, or—most frequently—the bureaucratic status quo.[6] Many projects are set up in such a way that they inevitably antagonize established agencies that have, or used to have, responsibilities in the activity which the new project, or rather the agency administering it, now claims as its preserve.

Some projects will be comparatively free from these hazards: for example, existing agencies are not likely to be too disturbed by a project whose activity is wholly new to the country—airline or large-scale electric power generation—or, even better, by a spatially isolated project—a new port or a big dam.[7] But take, at the opposite pole, a project that is affected by product uncertainty: such a project starts out with so broad a mission that many existing agencies feel threatened by it and will often do their best to paralyze it. In many ways this is the story of

6. Only the last case will be dealt with here. The San Lorenzo irrigation project is a good example of a project disturbing the social status quo; see below, pp. 59–60. For the ability of projects to undermine the political status quo, see Chap. 4.

7. In terms of concepts to be introduced in the next chapter, one might say that agencies set up to develop "site-bound" projects are not too likely to step on the toes of pre-existing agencies.

the Damodar Valley Corporation (DVC) which was set up in 1948, in the aftermath of the disastrous 1943 flood, amidst the emotions of Independence, to promote the "unified development of the resources of the Damodar Valley."[8] The corporation was endowed, along TVA lines, with a high degree of administrative autonomy from both the central government and the state governments of West Bengal and Bihar within which the valley is located. With the return of "normalcy," both the central and the state governments did their best to recover the powers they had handed over to DVC in a moment of euphoria. A particularly long and bitter feud developed in the 1950's between the corporation and the state of West Bengal, with DVC's part-time chairmen, who were mostly retired—and tired—civil servants, being no match for Dr. B. C. Roy, one of the great figures of the Independence Movement, a close friend of Nehru, and Chief Minister of West Bengal from 1948 to his death in 1962. As a result of these various conflicts, urgently required investment decisions were blocked or delayed, and partly wasteful competition arose between DVC and the states in electric power generation. Finally it became necessary to reorganize the agency with a view to redefining the responsibilities for electric power generation and to devolving some of its functions, notably irrigation and soil conservation, wholly upon the states; meanwhile the central government had already reentered the picture as final arbiter of water releases from DVC's multipurpose reservoirs. Thus, DVC's responsibilities, prestige, and morale were gradually cut down; in view of the strength and persistence of the assault against it, the surprising thing is actually not that it had to renounce many of its early ambitions, but that it survived at all. Survival was probably due to the sound instinct of the

8. For an excellent account of its early history, see Henry C. Hart, *New India's Rivers* (Bombay: Orient Longmanns, 1956), Chap. 4.

corporation to concentrate its activities, once the major river dams were built, on the construction and operation of large thermoelectric stations: by acquiring an impressive capability in this technically complex, high priority sector, the corporation retreated, as it were, to a position from which it could not be dislodged without great risk.

It is worth noting that administrative sequences exactly opposite to that of the Damodar Valley Corporation have been traced out by other agencies. Thailand's Royal Irrigation Department (RID) and El Salvador's Lempa River Hydroelectric Commission (CEL) both started with specific, limited tasks: the Royal Irrigation Department was founded in 1904 and during several decades concentrated all its efforts on irrigation and navigation in Thailand's Central Plain; the Lempa River Hydroelectric Commission was founded in 1945 with the exclusive purpose, as its name indicates, of building a large hydroelectric station on the Lempa, El Salvador's major river. In performing these tasks, both agencies acquired considerable technical and administrative expertise—as well as political connections—and subsequently were able to branch out into new areas of activity: El Salvador's CEL built additional hydro stations as well as a thermal station at the port of Acajutla; it came to assist with the financing of local distribution companies in the provinces and in 1962 stepped into retail distribution with a pilot project of rural or, rather, village electrification. In doing so, CEL "took on" for the first time the private company, CAESS, which since the establishment of CEL had been relegated to the distribution end of the power business, but which was intent on maintaining its exclusive rights to retail distribution in its wide concession area in and around San Salvador.

Thailand's Royal Irrigation Department has an even more impressive career of gradual expansion; in fact, it has become something of a "kingdom within a kingdom" as it branched out from irrigation of the Central Plain to all other parts of the country where irrigation was feasible, and from irrigation to the production of electric power, cement, fertilizer, not to mention the many operations ancillary to its irrigation activities such as agricultural experiment stations, the "largest machine shop in South East Asia," etc. These expansions were achieved with remarkable smoothness, the only upset being RID's eventual loss of control over the Yanhee Electricity Authority which it spawned.

Both the CEL and the RID experiences suggest that a good way for an agency to become multipurpose is to be first securely and competently grounded in one purpose. Starting out with a specific task, the agency uses the task to make itself strong enough to overcome the inevitable opposition that will arise when it finally does spread out into functions that overlap those of existing agencies. An agency like the Damodar Valley Corporation that is loudly multipurpose from the start, on the other hand, will have much greater trouble holding on to such functions.

The Damodar experience, supported by similar observations in Ethiopia, Ecuador, and Peru which it would be too long to relate, permits perhaps one generalization: At the moment of the creation of a new agency there is a tendency to underestimate the ability of the offended old-time bureaucracy to stage in due time a serious counteroffensive against the newcomer. The likelihood of this type of "backlash" is ignored or lightly and dangerously dismissed. But apart from this conclusion, not too much should be made of the Damodar Valley Corporation's "failure." In the first place, it could hardly have been foreseen at Independence that the states would gain as much in power within the Indian Union as they actually did, nor that DVC would acquire as formidable a foe as Dr. B. C. Roy. After all, interagency fights have also been known to end in victories for new agencies which, in that case, emerge with increased health and vigor. Moreover, it often happens that certain activities can only be initiated by disrupting the existing bureaucratic structure; in time, these activities can be handed over without harm to the older agencies as was done with irrigation, soil conservation, and reservoir regulation by DVC. Strangely enough, this sort of handing on is celebrated as a great triumph when it occurs between the public and the private sectors—as, for example, when the controlling interest in the Karnaphuli Paper Mill was sold in 1958 by the official Pakistan Industrial Development Corporation to Messrs. Dawood, the well-known industrialists; but it is often lamented and treated as a betrayal of hope when it happens, as for the Damodar Corporation, *within* the public sector.

We now come to a third type of administrative problems. The first type arose from within the project itself. The second resulted from features of project structure that gave or may have given offense to the established, "old-line" bureaucracy. Symmetry requires that the third type deal with aggressive actions originating outside and directed against the project agency. In other words, we are now interested in unprovoked and unjustified interferences, pressures, and "political takeovers." This third source of administrative trouble is actually so important a phenomenon that "insulation from politics" has become a principal objective in project administration. One popular way of insulating the project is to have it built and operated by a so-called "autonomous agency" (some aspects of this device will be discussed in Chapter 4). At this point, we are not interested so much in evaluating defensive measures as in understanding which projects are specially exposed to outside interferences. Some understanding of this differential vulnerability of projects is in fact a prerequisite for effective defensive measures.

The only kind of political interference we wish to discuss here is that penetration or takeover by parasitic forces that must be expected to occur occasionally in any country, and particularly in those where opportunities are strictly limited while the desire for rapid acquisition of wealth and power has suddenly become highly developed: in this environment a new project, equipped as it is with funds and jobs and consequently with opportunities for enrichment and for gaining political influence, is bound to excite a lot of appetites. Such projects are threatened with a fate similar to that of private firms in some underdeveloped countries that are subjected to arbitrary fiscal exactions from the powerholders as soon as they show signs of increased prosperity. Businessmen working under such conditions often belong to minority groups and have been aptly called "pariah entrepreneurs":[9] they expect and are fully prepared for such periodic plunders by the bureaucracy. We are interested in the corresponding phenomenon within the public sector itself. Here the plunder takes the form of the takeover of a project—sometimes from its start, sometimes at a later stage—by a purely self-serving political group. Poor or deteriorating performance in the construction and/or operation of the project can be expected to follow.[10]

Obviously the probability of such an occurrence depends on two factors: the appetites projects arouse and the built-in defenses they can muster. The principal defenses a project has are apparent technical complexity and a closely related property that might be called the elasticity of output with respect to competence and morale, i.e. the extent to which quantity and quality of output decline as a result of a given decline in

9. Riggs, *Administration in Developing Countries*, pp. 188–93.

10. It must be noted that we are not analyzing here the differential political appeal of projects or the political pressures behind them. We, rather, take it for granted that as a result of such pressures and of other factors, various projects are brought underway, and we are intent on exploring the differential vulnerability of projects to capture by parasitic groups.

staff competence or morale. It is clear, for example, that an electric power project, a telecommunications network, an airline, or a public health project simply cannot be staffed with the sole purpose of rewarding friends and extending one's political influence. This is rather less clear in railways: even though running a railway is in fact a very intricate business, the railways have lost much of the aura of scientific sophistication to more modern technologies so that it is often believed—quite wrongly—that they can be "taken over" with impunity. Highways and agricultural, irrigation, and educational projects have similarly weaker defenses than projects that boast the most advanced technology.

It follows that adding a highly technical dimension to a project will be useful in giving it some protection from political interference. For example, the position of Uruguay's Honorary Commission for livestock development vis-à-vis the Ministry of Agriculture was considerably strengthened by the addition to its activities of such scientific-technical pursuits as research on inoculants.

The rule that the activity with the most complex technology is best at repelling assaults of the hungry politicians is nicely illustrated in the case of Damodar Valley Corporation which lost all its nonpower activities—irrigation, soil conservation, and even flood control [11]—to the states or the central government and retained only the technologically complex power stations under its exclusive control.

The other factor in determining the vulnerability of projects to politically motivated interference and "takeovers" is the attractiveness of the project as a political and economic

11. In 1962 release of water from the reservoirs was made subject to the control of the Central Water and Power Commission after repeated complaints by the state of West Bengal about DVC practices, particularly in connection with the flood of 1959. Representatives of the central commission were stationed at Maithon Dam for this purpose.

power base. To some extent, every project—being a source of funds, jobs, and influence—is attractive in this way. As will be shown in the next section, a project that lacks a well-focused task, but is endowed with a fixed income (for example, through the earmarking of certain tax revenues), is particularly likely to be assaulted. In a general way, a distinction could perhaps be made between projects such as highways and hydroelectric stations that require only maintenance or minimal operation after construction, and those such as railways, irrigations, and thermoelectric stations that require a substantial flow of operating expenses for personnel and material inputs after construction. The latter should be a preferential target for parasitic appetites since they hold out the promise of indefinite enjoyment of the to-be-conquered benefits. This argument is not conclusive, however, for most would-be parasites have rather short-term horizons! Also, even when an individual project requires no operation, so that it no longer yields benefits once its construction is over, it may be undertaken by an organization that repeatedly builds such projects, so that a steady flow of benefits can be expected to accrue from its future construction activity. Hence, any highway department is just as attractive a target as the more operation-intensive projects.

Among the latter, one category deserves to be singled out as particularly likely to arouse appetites and to attract attention: projects that dispense *and can withhold* pretty much at will benefits representing a substantial part of the incomes of the beneficiaries. Here, control of the project would mean not only control over jobs and funds, but also power to influence, to dominate, and to exploit the groups depending on the project. In many projects, as most obviously in the case of roads, services cannot be withheld at the will of the project authorities. Irrigation projects, on the other hand, are particularly vulnerable to this kind of control (as are certain education and housing projects) : the irrigation farmers are indeed collectively and even individually dependent on the irrigation authorities—a fact that has provided Wittfogel with the basic element of his theory of the "despotic hydraulic society." It should be noted, however, that a technical advance, namely the introduction of overhead irrigation under pressure, changes the situation fundamentally: with this most advanced system, the individual irrigation farmer no longer must agree with the authorities on a certain quantity of water for certain days; water is now available at all times "on demand" upon the turning of a faucet, and the irrigation farmer is hardly more dependent on the irrigation authorities than the city dweller on the city waterworks administration.

In sum, the differential vulnerability of projects to disturbances from without seems to depend more on their defenses (such as technological complexity) than on fundamental differences in their attractiveness to would-be parasites.

Supply Uncertainties: Finance

It may seem strange that we have not mentioned so far what is commonly considered one of the major hazards faced by development projects: the possibility that they may stay uncompleted because the needed funds fail to become available. Certainly, in many developing countries there is much visual evidence of stalled construction, and when the visitor asks for a reason, the most common answer is precisely that the project ran out of money.

While the limitation of our survey to World Bank projects obviously reduces the incidence of financial uncertainty, the reason this factor is given limited attention is that to a very considerable extent it is a mere reflection of other problems. Many financial difficulties of projects derive from unexpectedly arising technical obstacles, and others will clearly be due to such matters as low efficiency caused by intergroup conflict. Thus, by analyzing these difficulties and the area of their most likely incidence, we have by the same token dealt with the possible emergence of financial problems in the course of project construction and operation.

But financial uncertainty can also arise out of the economic, institutional, and political environment within which projects function in developing countries, and to that extent even projects that are untroubled in every other respect could be affected. This "external" financial uncertainty is due to two principal factors: (a) the policy makers' fickleness and second thoughts—frequently, but not invariably, caused by a change in political leadership—which may cause them to withhold promised funds or to divert funds already set aside for the project to other uses; and (b) inflation which erodes the real value of appropriated funds and therefore makes it necessary to confirm over and over again, by making fresh funds available, the decision to undertake the project and to push ahead with it.

In a sense, inflation is a mechanism that makes it easy for decision makers to indulge in fickleness and to act upon whatever second thoughts they may have; for what takes an overt and aggressive act of breaking a promise, or of taking money away from a project under conditions of stable prices, is accomplished by simple inaction when inflationary conditions prevail.[12]

What kinds of projects are most likely to become victims of fickleness and second thoughts? In the first place it is obvious that well managed and powerfully backed projects have a better chance of coming through these tests unscathed. But

12. This effect of inflation on investment decisions is stressed in Judith D. Tendler, *The Rise of Public Power in Brazil* (to be published in 1968 by Harvard University Press), Chap. 5.

this observation does not permit identification of the kinds of projects that are particularly exposed to financial uncertainty. For that purpose, another distinction is of greater interest: some projects will suffer little damage if they are interrupted; in fact, a road of which only a segment has been built may have a limited usefulness pending the completion of the whole project. Such projects are obviously easier to interrupt and therefore more likely "victims" than those, like a dam, that not only must be completed if they are to be of any use, but cry out to be finished lest the effort already invested be wholly lost. These matters will be treated in the next chapter under the heading of "temporal latitude"; it will therefore suffice here to say that temporal latitude invites the kind of financial uncertainty we have been discussing.

Since political instability and strenuous competition for pathetically limited public funds are characteristic of many less developed countries, "external" financial uncertainty has been so prominent an evil that various attempts have been made to "abolish" it. One device, widely used—for example, in Ecuador—is the earmarking of the revenue from a special tax, or of some set percentage of total tax revenue, for the project or activity whose budget one wishes to protect. In this fashion, the attempt to escape from one evil, fiscal inconstancy, has often led policy makers into another, namely the utter destruction of the unity of the budget. More interesting from our point of view, experience with the earmarking device has revealed that external financial uncertainty is by no means always an evil. As has already been intimated, it can act as an incentive for good performance while the assurance of a prebend regardless of performance may well stimulate appetites for a parasitic takeover.

That fiscal uncertainty can lead to good performance while fiscal sinecure invites parasitism is illustrated by the experiences of two development agencies in Brazil's Northeast.[13] Among the projects forming the basis of the present study, the uneven career of the Guayas Highway Committee, which disposed of a safe revenue from gasoline and other taxes, tells a similar story. But perhaps it is not necessary to dwell unduly on the point that for a project, as for a person, an assured income is by no means a sufficient condition for achievement and may on the contrary fundamentally impair it.

Excess Demand

Turning now to uncertainties and difficulties related to the demand side, we shall first examine the less common and less recognized problem, namely excess demand. Some examples will make clear that the danger we have in mind is not an ordinary excess of demand over supply, which could be ended by an increase in price, but one that arises out of more insidious situations and results in conflicts over project benefits.

The San Lorenzo irrigation scheme in northern Peru consists in a diversion of the waters of the Quiroz River toward tablelands lying between the Piura and Chira rivers. The original expectation was that 50,000 hectares of these quasi-desertic lands could be irrigated by the diverted waters, the remainder of which were to be emptied into the Lower Piura whose valley plantations have long been famous for cultivation of long-staple "Pima" cotton. For a number of reasons, several years elapsed between the completion of the irrigation works and the actual start of irrigation in the San Lorenzo area; during this period all of the diverted Quiroz waters, nicely regulated by the newly built San Lorenzo reservoir, were available in the Lower Piura Valley and served to increase the land under cot-

13. The São Francisco Valley Commission (CVSF) and the São Francisco Hydroelectric Company (CHESF), respectively. See my *Journeys Toward Progress*, pp. 50–58.

ton cultivation. When finally the San Lorenzo scheme in the tablelands got underway, it was realized that if the waters were to be used for their original purpose, they would have to be withdrawn to some extent from use on the Lower Piura plantations, possibly causing a shrinkage in cotton acreage. Naturally this was not a pleasant prospect for the plantation owners who were, moreover, worried about the impact of the irrigation project on their labor supply and perhaps, more generally, about the "demonstration effect" of a different and unheard of pattern of land tenure and agriculture—small, owner-operated farms growing a number of crops, in addition to the traditional cotton. Thus, when plans were finally made in 1963 for the full development of the project, the economically and politically powerful Piura landowners organized a determined opposition; the ardently reformist managers of the project were equally spoiling for a fight. The emerging conflict would of course largely vanish if additional water resources were to become available and, for this reason, the attention of those who looked for a nonantagonistic way out of the dilemma centered on the possibilities—presently under study—of either raising water through tubewells in the Piura Valley or of diverting waters from yet another river, the Chira, into the San Lorenzo-Piura region.

Our next example of excess demand or conflict over benefits comes from India where the limited water volume of the Damodar River also gave rise to conflict among different users. Industrial and urban demand for water in the Durgapur area increased much faster than anticipated and threatened to reduce the availability of water for such originally contemplated uses as irrigation and navigation that were being developed less rapidly or not at all. Hopeful of eventually catching up with the original plans, the authorities in charge of these activities (irrigation in particular) were not ready to relinquish what they considered their fair share; new claims were also staked from other quarters when it was realized that the silting up of the Lower Damodar consequent upon the expanding up-river uses of its waters called for the administration of periodic "flushing doses." These conflicting demands contributed to the tension between the Damodar Valley Corporation and the state of West Bengal and to a weakening of the DVC's authority symbolized by the appointment of representatives from the central government who were to watch over the releases of water from the DVC reservoirs.[14] As in San Lorenzo, various plans to increase the available waters of the Damodar by new diversion schemes were also canvassed.

The peculiarity of the situations just illustrated is: (1) that the supply of the resource (water) that is being made available is strictly limited, at least in the short run; and (2) that the users fall into several distinct groups who are likely to fight for what they consider their fair share of the waters by means of political actions instead of letting rational principles of allocation prevail. One reason is that such principles are by no means easy to make out: in both San Lorenzo and the Damodar Valley the benefits of making water available for different purposes to different groups comprised important social and political dimensions that are difficult to quantify.

For project managers plagued by excess capacity it is impossible to conceive of a pleasanter situation than a demand for the output of their project that outruns the supply. It is clear, however, that in the situations depicted here, excess demand can be quite uncomfortable for the project managers and, more important, can offset through social and political conflict and crisis much of the economic benefit produced by the project. On the other hand, if the conflict is happily resolved, the project will have brought the additional benefit of providing an object-lesson in constructive conflict-solving.

14. As noted above, p. 54.

In any event, it is important for project planners (wishing to dispense with the Hiding Hand) to be aware of this category of risks. Its locus is most typically the irrigation project because of the limitations on the supply of water—which, though not absolute, are nevertheless more rigid than in other projects. In electric power or roads, for example, it is clear to all, in case demand presses on supply, that new power plants can be built or that the roadbed can be widened. Temporary shortages and bottlenecks may arise, but even then the conflict among various groups of would-be consumers is unlikely to reach the same intensity as that typical of irrigation projects; and the energies of these groups are more likely to be spent on constructive joint action and pressures to get new capacity built than on fighting over the size of the individual slices of a pie whose total volume is presumed to be fixed.

Projects other than irrigation can nevertheless be affected by a quite similar phenomenon: a project may raise expectations that its services will be made available to a group that is not among its intended or even possible beneficiaries, and this group will then stake a claim for a share in the project's output that cannot be granted.

The excess demand of this situation is rather *sui generis* but the conflict and frustration resulting from it are no less real. Electric power projects appear to be good candidates for falling into this particular trap. In Uganda, the national electric power agency (Uganda Electricity Board—UEB), in search of new customers, undertook in the late fifties and in the sixties to build transmission lines to the various provincial towns or administrative centers as well as to coffee mills, cotton gins, and tea factories. But with power newly available in the towns and with transmission lines conspicuously transporting it overhead through the countryside, many nearby villagers thought that it would be a simple matter to supply them too and so petitioned the UEB. Some of them even went so far as to hopefully hang lightbulbs from their ceilings! Unfortunately, because the farmers' settlements were scattered and their prospective consumption very low, any large-scale extension of the distribution network into the countryside would be totally uneconomical [15] and out of the question for the UEB which to this date has never turned in a profit. Since, on the other hand, Uganda's so-called towns are little more than administrative and commercial centers almost exclusively inhabited by civil servants and East Indian traders, the UEB's transmission lines served essentially to make the rich and powerful more comfortable.

There were of course many things to be said in favor of the project, from the need to find a market for UEB's excess capacity to the opening up of opportunities for small industry in the towns; but the awakening of demands for rural electrification that cannot be fulfilled for a long time, and the consequent tensions, must here be entered as a social cost. In Uganda this cost stood out with special sharpness as it risked widening one of the country's most dangerous ethnic cleavages, that between the Africans and the East Indians.

There are of course other types of projects that are apt to elicit this sort of unsatisfiable demand and hence lead to resentments in the groups that feel frustrated in their newly aroused hopes for progress. Irrigation projects frequently are under considerable pressure to cover a wider area than is justified on strict productivity criteria, given the volume of water that is available.[16] Education, health, housing, and water sup-

15. The UEB stood ready to bring power to the villages in the vicinity of the towns it supplied, provided the villagers made an adequate capital contribution to the cost of the transmission, step-down transformers, and distribution. But since power was brought to the towns (and therefore to the East Indians) wholly at UEB's expense, this policy was resented as rank discrimination against Africans.

16. For an examination of such criteria, see H. G. Van der Tak and J. K. Schmedtje, *Economic Aspects of Water Utilization in Irrigation Projects* (International Bank for Reconstruction and Development, Report EC–132, 1965), Chaps. 3 and 5.

ply projects with their limited capacity and their wide appeal are other examples. Unlike the Uganda case, however, programs in these sectors can be so designed as to avoid the impression that any important group is systematically excluded from their benefits.

Transportation is comparatively immune from the particular problem we have discussed, because of the very elastic capacity especially of highways and, to a lesser extent, of other modes. While it is not always possible for a person living close to a transmission line to get a power connection or for one who lives near a hospital to be admitted there, a new road can normally accommodate for a lengthy period all the demands for traffic originating in the area it traverses. This immunity to the problem of unsatisfiable excess demand is grounded in a technical characteristic peculiar to highways: the demand—the traffic volume—they are able to handle is far larger than that for which they are designed. This characteristic is not, however, an unmixed blessing: while highways do not summarily reject excess demand and do not therefore cause immediate hostility and unhappiness, they are liable to deteriorate as a result of accommodating that demand—at least in the absence of stepped up maintenance—and this deterioration will disgruntle the users so that unhappiness and resentment appear here also, even though in a delayed and perhaps more constructive form.

Thus, in Ecuador, the highway from Guayaquil to Empalme and Quevedo, built in the early fifties by the highway committee of Guayas Province, was to be one of several roads designed to open up the coastal flatlands around Guayaquil. It turned unexpectedly into the country's essential artery, not only because it became the principal connection between Ecuador's two largest cities, Quito and Guayaquil, but even more because it carried an ever rising share of the country's then rapidly increasing banana crop. Not having been built to accommodate this extremely heavy traffic, the highway was soon in a very poor state of repair, and thus the Guayas committee was brought into disrepute by its most successful project; largely as a result, it lost some of the autonomous powers with which it had originally been endowed.

Excess demand, then, does not seem to be an exceptional happening, nor is it wholly innocuous. Essentially, the emergence of excess demand implies that some hopes that have been aroused by a project must be frustrated; no wonder, then, that excess demand can cause serious conflict and sociopolitical damage.

Inadequate Demand

One reason the risks of excess demand receive less attention than they deserve may be that the damage—group conflict, frustration, hostility—they inflict is felt only in part by the project and the project agency; to a considerable extent, these ill-effects are external to the project and tend therefore to be neglected by the project planners. The situation is substantially different for the dangers of inadequate demand or excess capacity that impair directly the financial position or at least the prestige of the project; these dangers are therefore very much on the minds of project planners and operators.

Inadequate demand was experienced by the projects in our sample in very different forms and degrees. From the point of view of differential exposure of projects to this risk it is useful first to distinguish between three basic situations: (a) existence of effective demand (at remunerative prices) for the project's output is known to predate the project's completion; (b) on the contrary, emergence of such demand is fully expected to lag behind the project's completion; (c) the demand is expected to arise more or less at the time the project is ready to yield its output.

The first case, with demand firmly in existence by the time the project is completed, is characteristic of the following types of activities: projects leading to import-substitution such as, among our projects, the Karnaphuli Paper Mill; projects whose output will be exported and will add only a comparatively small amount to world supply, as will the additional beef and wool production that is to result from the Uruguayan project for pasture improvement; and projects producing goods or services in which backlog demands have already accumulated, as occurs frequently in so-called infrastructural investments in the wake of rapid industrial and urban growth. An ideal example here is Ethiopia's telecommunications, since the postwar expansion started out essentially as reconstruction of the previous Italian-installed system which had badly deteriorated during and immediately after the war. In all of these cases uncertainty about demand, or the risk of inadequate demand, was at a minimum.

Two of our electric power projects, in El Salvador and in the Damodar Valley, could also qualify as infrastructural investments designed largely to remedy a pre-existing shortage, but in both cases the additions to the supply due to the new plants (30,000 kilowatts at El Salvador's Rio Lempa hydroelectric station, and 150,000 kilowatts at the Damodar Corporation's Bokaro thermoelectric station) were so large in relation to the market served that some excess capacity existed during the first years of their operation. This situation led to a typical cobweb sequence transposed to the public sector: when the project managers pressed for the next expansion, the existence of excess capacity in the past was seized upon to justify delay; as a result, excess capacity was soon followed once again by a period of power shortage. This was particularly disastrous in India, first because a power shortage in Calcutta implies serious loss of production and employment; and, secondly, from the point of view of the Damodar Corporation, because the agency's inability to supply needed power became a key factor (or pretext) in the decision of Bihar and particularly West Bengal to compete with DVC through power installations of their own. In this case, then, the penalty for temporary excess capacity was far stiffer than loss of revenue: it was, through a sequence of events, the encroachment of the states on the DVC's functions in electric power generation and a somewhat wasteful duplication of administration, skilled personnel, and capital equipment in the power sector.[17] Such can be the hazards of overreacting.

Next to the situations where demand is known to antedate the completion of projects are those where demand is known not to exist but is expected to be elicited gradually by the physical existence of the project and by its readiness to pour forth its outputs. This concept of "building ahead of demand" is well known from the development literature, but has by now been rather battered by critical assaults in which I have taken part.[18] The latest and perhaps most damaging blow has been struck by a detailed demonstration that what was thought to be the most celebrated historical instance of "building ahead of demand," namely the "opening up" of the United States through railroad building in the mid-nineteenth century, was in effect a rather cautious, step-by-step undertaking in which emerging demand was fairly correctly "smelled out" and re-

17. The crassest case of such duplication was the establishment of West Bengal's thermoelectric plant at Durgapur with an initial capacity of 60,000 kilowatts at less than two miles from the DVC's thermal plant, in spite of a provision in the DVC Act that prohibits generation of "electrical energy at an installation having an aggregate capacity of more than 10,000 kilowatts in any part of the Damodar Valley." Cited in R. E. Hamilton, *The Damodar Valley Corporation: India's Experiment with the TVA Idea* (unpublished doctoral dissertation, Duke University, 1966), p. 251.

18. *Strategy of Economic Development*, Chap. 5.

sponded to by the railroad companies.[19] Of course, by the
time the notion of building infrastructure ahead of demand as
a key to development had been debunked, it had done considerable damage. Many of the African railways, for example,
were built by colonial governments with the idea that the
"American experience" could be easily duplicated. Actually,
besides the fact that, as we now know, the American experience was being erroneously invoked, the railroad planners for
Africa overlooked a crucial technological feature. In the areas
where railroads had been successful—in Europe, the Americas,
and India—there existed draft animals and wheeled traffic that
made it possible to transport bulky merchandise from and to
the railheads over considerable distances; in most of tropical
Africa, on the other hand, human porterage was the only
means of transport so that the area "opened up" by an African
railroad consisted of a far narrower band on both sides of the
tracks than elsewhere.[20] This situation changed only with the
automotive age whose advent was, however, a very mixed
blessing for the railroads, since the truck-highway complex
became rapidly and preponderantly a competitive rather than
a complementary mode.

Railroad building in Africa thus suffered from two disabili-
ties: it was undertaken on the basis of a misinterpretation of
successful foreign railroad experience, and it failed to recognize
the specific factor that would make the duplication of this
experience in Africa very difficult.

A rather similar situation arose with respect to the only one
of our projects whose construction was explicitly based on the
building-ahead-of-demand strategy: the Owen Falls Hydroelectric Station in Uganda which suffered for years from con-

19. Albert Fishlow, *American Railroads and the Transformation of the
Ante-Bellum Economy* (Harvard University Press, 1965), Chaps. 4 and 8.
20. See S. D. Neumark, *Foreign Trade and Economic Development in
Africa,* Food Research Institute (Stanford University, 1964), p. 75.

siderable excess capacity. This project also was advocated because foreign experience allegedly had demonstrated that supply of power creates its own demand.[21] Again, the specific adverse conditions under which the electric power industry was going to operate in a country like Uganda went largely unrecognized; in particular, the wide geographic scatter of the African population, in conjunction with its low purchasing power, assured that "bringing power to Uganda" and "reaching down to the African through a country-wide distribution network" meant in effect for many years supplying power primarily to a very limited group of civil servants, expatriates, and East Indians.

The current discredit of the building-ahead-of-demand strategy as well as the requirements laid down by national and international financing institutions have resulted in most projects being presented as though demand would arise more or less simultaneously with the availability of the new supply of goods and services due to the project. In fact, there is of course a category of projects where considerable excess capacity is likely to exist for a long initial period, irrigation projects being a prime example; the lag of utilization of the waters made available takes different forms and has widely different reasons, yet it always seems to happen, whether the water merely supplements rainfall (India) or river overflow (Thailand), or

21. The following quote is representative: "Power, however produced, represents a small fraction of production costs in any industry, but the replacement of wood by electricity as a source of power over this considerable part of Uganda would probably be followed by many developments which are difficult to foresee. Experience with electricity in other parts of the world has nearly always shown that the most optimistic estimates of consumption have been greatly exceeded soon after the provision of a reliable and cheap supply." E. B. Worthington, "A Development Plan for Uganda," quoted in Appendix VII of *Government of Uganda Owen Falls Hydroelectric Scheme Project Report* by Sir Alexander Gibbs & Partners and Kennedy & Donkin (January 1948).

whether prior to the scheme no cropping at all or only wheat cultivation was possible, as in Peru and southern Italy, respectively.

The expression "building ahead of demand" does not do very well, however, at catching the reality of these situations. It evokes a slow, but gradual and fairly steady, swelling of entrepreneurial and other demands for the services offered by the project. In irrigation, on the other hand, the road to full utilization often requires the solving of organizational problems and of technological uncertainty about the crops it is possible to grow and the removal of market uncertainty with respect to these crops. Utilization is therefore more a matter of administrative, technological, and marketing *problem-solving* that must be engaged in after the irrigation structures are in place, than of the simple picking up of clearly existing profitable opportunities by entrepreneurs who become gradually aware of them.

It could of course be strongly argued that administrative, crop, and marketing problems should have been solved before the irrigation works were undertaken; for one thing, if they are real problems, some of them might never be solved and the irrigation project would be a permanent failure. Nevertheless, the trouble with the prescription is that it may simply not be possible to solve the problems we have been talking about *in advance*, that is, without first building the irrigation works. The organizational ability of irrigation authorities to settle the right farmers properly on the land and to create a climate of cooperation and mutual trust can only be acquired "by doing"; by bringing in water in trucks, experimental stations could (and should) investigate which crops will do well in the to-be-irrigated area, but there is no certainty about the subsequent ability and willingness of the irrigation farmers to follow the resulting advice; and market studies for agricultural products cannot replace the actual test of the "live" market. Hence irrigation implies *sequential* problem-solving. Prior studies and advance planning cannot change this basic fact; they have the very important tasks of shortening the time interval between the various sequential steps that are required and of lowering the risks involved in taking these steps.

It should perhaps be added—at the risk of weakening our preceding argument—that one reason for the "sequentiality" of irrigation projects is that in many countries one finds considerably more pressure, enthusiasm, and competence for the engineering phase of irrigation projects than for their agricultural and marketing tasks. Such an "imbalance" might be corrected by bringing research and training efforts to bear on these neglected areas; but on occasion the only faintly promising device is to build the irrigation works first. With the thorn of underutilized capacity in their side, the irrigation authorities, even when they were not originally responsible for the agricultural side, will feel a strong incentive to organize not only efficient agricultural and marketing research, but to become involved in the actual growing and selling phases of the project. In our Peruvian, Italian, and Thai irrigation projects, this mechanism, akin to what we have called forward linkage in the process of industrialization, was clearly at work.[22]

The lag between completion of the project and the emergence of capacity-filling demand must therefore be expected in projects where this emergence is a matter of sequential problem-solving, whether in the sense that problem B cannot be solved at all until A is in place or in the sense that problem

22. A mechanism similar to backward linkage can also be observed in irrigation and hydroelectric projects using storage dams. Once the dam is built, efforts will get underway to preserve the reservoir's capacity by preventing its silting up. In this way soil conservation and other anti-erosion programs will be actively undertaken after the dam is built. This sequence was observed in the Damodar Valley as well as in El Salvador.

B is unlikely to be tackled energetically until the being in place of A has created a party with a vital stake in solving B.

We suggest, then, that with this sort of rationale it is possible to rehabilitate certain types of temporary excess capacity or lags of demand behind the completion of projects. At the same time, the analysis points to the need for care in designing institutions in such a manner that excess capacity will motivate the project operators to search actively for customers or, rather, to solve the production and marketing problems forestalling full utilization. For example, when considerable authority is delegated to the local manager of an irrigation project, he is likely to identify with the success of the project as a whole and to become involved therefore in the "next" phases, that is, those following the construction of the irrigation structures; on the contrary, if the irrigation activities of a wide area are handled centrally, the purely engineering outlook is likely to prevail. Similar institutional conclusions could be drawn for the case of penetration roads and the subsequent settlement of new lands: here the tie-in between the building and maintenance of the roads and the next phases of agricultural production and marketing is normally more tenuous than in irrigation, and it is therefore even more important to design institutions that will foster such a tie-in, through decentralization and other incentives.

Having discussed first the case where demand for a project's capacity output is likely to be adequate because backlog demand has accumulated (or because demand is infinitely elastic) and then the situations in which excess capacity is fully expected for some time after construction, we must now consider the "normal" case where demand for the project's capacity output will providentially arise at just about the time the newly built project is ready to yield it. This case may be considered normal because most new investment is made in anticipation of concurrent growth in domestic or foreign demands.

The risk of a shortfall in demand depends on the accuracy of these expectations. Once again, our interest lies in differentiating between sectors and projects, this time on the basis of the reliability of expectations about new demand emerging as a result of the growth process. Clearly for some types of projects this reliability is quite high or, put differently, the margin of error affecting the estimate of future buying decisions by firms and individuals is quite low; an obvious example would be a project for expansion of electric power generation in a large interconnected area with growing cities and industries; or a project increasing marketable basic food output in a country with a growing population. In other words, projects run least risk of being stuck with excess capacity when demand for their output is linked to the expected *total* growth experience of the country rather than to any regional, sectoral, or other narrower segment of the economy.

The matter can be put more precisely in terms of input-output analysis: the risk of excess capacity is lowest when the project's output is widely spread as an input over many sectors (and regions) or when output goes overwhelmingly to final mass consumption demand; the risk is the bigger the greater is the concentration of the project's output on a few final consumers or on a few cells of the interindustry matrix. It is largely for the case when this concentration is considerable and the risk of inadequate demand correspondingly high that the concepts of "balanced growth" and "mutually supporting investments" have been evolved. The idea here is that when we are sufficiently unsure about the demand for the project's output arising of its own accord, the planners must make sure that it does so by causing the appropriate investment decisions to be taken.

It looks therefore as though we really did not have much to worry about. For either, so it seems, we deal with a sector in which the reliability of the demand forecast is high; or, when that reliability is low, we employ a technique that will force the demand to show up. Unfortunately, there are at least two strong reasons why the world falls rather short of being so comfortable a place.

In the first place, the two kinds of projects that have been discussed do not exhaust the universe of possible cases. There is surely a third category where neither of the two favorable conditions prevails: demand for the project's output is neither reliable nor is it enforceable through coordinated investment planning.

This category includes the types of projects discussed in connection with the concept of "building ahead of demand," such as penetration roads or irrigation projects: here the demand for the water or the transport services of the road is uncertain because of supply and marketing uncertainty surrounding the crops that farmers are to produce with the help of these inputs. And demand is not enforceable because in most societies farmers cannot be forced to migrate in the same manner as one can make sure—or believes he can—that an electric power station will have some large industrial customers. True enough, customers for the roads or water can be coaxed through credit measures and technical assistance; or, in the irrigation case, they can in addition be penalized for nonuse of water through appropriately designed land or water taxes. But all these measures will be unavailing if the crucial supply and marketing uncertainties are not solved, and as we have seen, there can be no real advance assurance on these matters.

These drawbacks of projects with both unreliable and unenforceable demand go some way toward explaining the backseat they usually take as well as the setbacks they often suffer once they are undertaken. Especially after a few setbacks, investors and planners will tend to stay away from this type of uncertainty-ridden project in agriculture and natural resources, thus creating that well-known imbalance in the economy that comes from concentration on the urban-industrial complex.

We took an overly sanguine view of our present subject matter for another reason: in subdividing conceivable projects into those with reliable demand and those in which demand can be assured through coordinated investment planning (including coordination of, say, only two projects) we accepted the claims of the latter technique too much at face value. If we are serious about the pervasive nature of the various supply uncertainties discussed earlier in this chapter, then the erection of a "mutually supporting" complex is going to be a rather more risky affair than its advocates have realized. But to appreciate properly this point a brief digression will be helpful.

Digression: The R&D Strategy

Unlike demand uncertainties (especially the danger of insufficient demand) which have always received considerable attention, the substantial technological and administrative uncertainties harbored by the supply side of projects have not been adequately acknowledged and mapped out. If it were recognized that many projects are in effect voyages of technological and administrative discovery, would that change any important procedures of project planning and implementation? It might. In the United States, analysis of the research and development (R&D) process has produced some interesting generalizations and suggestions about the methods of organization that should be adopted when both the goal to be reached and the path to that goal are highly uncertain, as they typically are when new products or processes are to be developed. Since we have contended that the R&D component of development projects is larger than is commonly realized, it is useful to summarize briefly the outcome of the discussion on appropriate R&D strategies and then to examine whether these strategies are applicable to the process of project planning and implementation.

In the late fifties, a group of economists of the RAND Corporation investigated in detail the research and development process characteristic of new weapons systems. While the impetus for these studies originated in the wide, and widely noted, discrepancies between estimated and actual cost and time spent for the procurement of various items, the analysts soon went beyond this rather narrow frame of reference and arrived at some unorthodox general ideas about the "conditions for R&D progress."[23]

The premises of these ideas are essentially two: (1) the goal of the R&D planner is not uniquely set; he is interested in a new product that outperforms present products in several respects or dimensions, but there is a wide range of performance characteristics that would be satisfactory to him; moreover, he does not attempt to ascertain the most desirable combination of characteristics until a product with such characteristics has actually been developed and tested; (2) on the way to his goal range, the R&D planner faces very large un-

23. See papers by B. H. Klein, T. A. Marschak, A. W. Marshall, W. H. Meckling, and R. R. Nelson in *The Rate and Direction of Inventive Activity* (Princeton University Press, 1962); R. R. Nelson, "Uncertainty, Learning and the Economics of Parallel R and D," *Review of Economics and Statistics*, Vol. 43 (November 1961), pp. 351–64, and "The Efficient Achievement of Rapid Technological Progress," *American Economic Review*, Vol. 56 (May 1966), pp. 232–41. For an attempt to show points of contact of these writings with thought on economic development and on the policy-making process, see A. O. Hirschman and C. E. Lindblom, "Economic Development, Research and Development, and Policy-Making: Some Converging Views," *Behavioral Science*, Vol. 7 (April 1962), pp. 211–22.

certainties, and one of his principal concerns must be the reduction of these uncertainties or the "buying of information" before he commits the bulk of his funds.

These premises resulted in a series of policy prescriptions that differ sharply from conventional optimizing techniques applied to ordinary production processes:

1. Rigid specifications of the performance characteristics of the desired product should be avoided for fear of excluding a product that is perhaps no less desirable, and far more feasible, than some other.

2. When the desired product is a "system" containing several components, there should similarly be no rigid stipulation in advance about the way in which the components are to be adjusted to each other as it is important to give each team working on a component the maximum freedom of movement even though subsequently a special effort will have to be made to fit the various pieces of the system together.

3. In considering alternative approaches to developing the desired product or its components, the correct procedure is not necessarily to decide which is the best prospective approach on the basis of the most sophisticated benefit-cost analysis available; in view of the large uncertainties surrounding all approaches at an early stage of R&D, it may be advisable to try out in practice several approaches until the uncertainties have been sufficiently reduced and to delay until then the decision as to the best approach. The cost of developing several prototypes may be less than the cost of developing only one whose prospects look best at an early stage, but whose production may then run into some gigantic snag because the more adverse among the large uncertainties have come into play.

Correct decision making in research and development is therefore sharply distinguished from decision making in known production processes: it is more flexible in its goal setting, it relies on multiple and parallel approaches, it is not rigidly coordinated, it is gradual and sequential in that both means and ends of the R&D process are frequently reviewed and modified in the light of newly acquired information.

From this brief sketch of the basic principles of the R&D strategy it is obvious that its tenets run directly counter to those of the balanced-growth or coordinated-investment strategy. The latter requires precisely that exact scheduling, prearranged dovetailing of components, and all-round certainty about both means and ends that is anathema to the former. Planning for an interdependent network of firms that will support each other in demand makes it almost necessary for the planners (if they are to sleep) to be blind to any evidence that some of the projects with which they are concerned require our voyages of technological and sociological discovery. Such blindness necessarily multiplies the risks and dangers arising from supply uncertainty. The interesting point about this clash of the R&D and balanced-growth strategies is that each was put forward to resolve one kind of uncertainty—the former, supply, and the latter, demand uncertainty.

The situation here described should in principle be familiar to opportunity-cost-conscious economists: an advance in one direction, namely the reduction of the risks resulting from demand uncertainties, is bought at a cost of larger risks due to supply uncertainties. And it may well be that the principle of increasing cost applies here also: beyond a certain point, policies aiming at the elimination of demand uncertainties would increase the potential damage that could be wrought by supply uncertainties to such an extent that the aggregate risk would be greater than before.

The same conclusion can be reached by setting out from a slightly different starting point. Central direction or coordination of investment planning has at times been advocated, not because of demand uncertainties, but because uncoordinated investment activity is said to proceed on the assumption by each firm that other firms will maintain an unchanged level of output. It can then be shown that this assumption will lead to undue timidity on the part of investors. For, given economies of scale, an increase in output by one firm in response to some surge in demand will lead to a decrease in its unit costs, and given interdependence, this decrease is likely to cause demand for the firm's output to expand beyond the initial surge. In such cases, then, the expansion originally scheduled by the firm will prove to be insufficient, "private profitability [of investment] understates its social desirability," and the economy will grow at a slower pace than it could and should.[24]

There is no doubt that the private investor may be affected by the sort of timidity and myopia implied by this argument. But two points need to be made. First, as a matter of historical fact, decentralized investment activity has on occasion been perfectly capable of taking scale and interdependence effects into account.[25] Secondly and more important in our context, when myopia does prevail, it may well be a blessing in disguise if the prospective investments are strongly affected by technological, administrative, and other supply uncertainties. These uncertainties are far more likely to be resolved rapidly and economically by successive smallish doses of investment, undertaken in response to prospective private profitability in one industry after another, than by a large simultaneous expansion of investment in several industries. The latter could easily result in the immobilization of large amounts of capital and, in fact, in a slower rate of growth of output than would be realized under conditions of myopia.[26]

24. I am referring to, and quoting from, Tibor Scitovsky's well-known article, "Two Concepts of External Economics," *Journal of Political Economy*, Vol. 62 (April 1954), p. 149.

25. Fishlow, *American Railroads*, p. 309.

26. To avoid misunderstanding, it should be added that the above argument is not meant as an attack on planning as such, but as a criticism of the kind of planning that ignores the existence of supply uncertainties.

Something of this kind may have happened to industrial development in India whose planners were much taken by the idea of building up concurrently several large-scale machinery plants which would be able to count on each other and on the expanding heavy industries in steel, electric power, and cement for an important portion of their output. Timetable breakdowns in the wake of individual projects' supply problems have in fact converted the process into a piecemeal or sequential (to use a term with a positive connotation) affair which, had it been *planned as such* from the start, would have been far less costly.[27]

A similar observation can sometimes be made for individual projects. The Karnaphuli Paper Mill was conceived as an "integrated" pulp and paper operation—integrated in the sense that aside from fuel, power, and some make-up chemicals it was to be self-sufficient, for it was to operate from the start with the local bamboo as basic raw material for pulping and it was equipped with a full chemical-recovery plant. But since the mill was in place before extraction of bamboo had been properly organized and before the chemical plant had been fully assembled, it ran for eighteen months largely on imported pulp and chemicals. By the time bamboo began to arrive in volume at the plant site, the various units of the chemical-recovery plant were ready, but their operation was crippled by the high silica content of the bamboo, as already reported. It was only after the problems caused by the silica had been successfully solved, some three years after the start of operations, that the mill was integrated in fact as well as in name. In view of this history, the financial results of the mill would have been better if the arrival of its various units had been staged,

27. See Edward S. Mason, *Economic Development in India and Pakistan*, Occasional Paper No. 13, Center for International Affairs, Harvard University, September 1966, pp. 6, 13.

that is, if the mill had aimed at something like the gradual integration it actually achieved. Naturally, it would have been even better if the bamboo had been ready for the mill when the mill was ready for it, and if there had been no problems with the chemical-recovery plant. But the likelihood of this optimal outcome was perhaps sufficiently small that it would have been worthwhile to consider the advisability of a second-best staged solution, for what we got in effect was a third-best solution, with virtually simultaneous erection of the integrated plant but severely staged operations that caused much of the capital equipment to stand idle during a prolonged period.

Mitigation of Uncertainties

This chapter had as its principal purpose an investigation of the uncertainties affecting projects and of the affinities of each uncertainty for various types of projects. Nevertheless, it was perhaps inevitable that we should end by discussing ways and means of mitigating these uncertainties. In fact, all we need to do for this purpose is to expand some previous remarks on this topic.

The most familiar idea is that it is possible to reduce uncertainty by paying the price of giving up the potentially most profitable course which, however, is also the riskiest one. Staged construction combined with staged import substitution, as just noted, would represent an application of this idea to project design on the supply side. On the demand side, a similar phenomenon can be observed. Just as the possibility of continuing to import some inputs from abroad permits a new industry to reconnoiter gradually its technological supply uncertainties, so the possibility of growing traditional crops with an assured market is of considerable help in reducing the uncertainties affecting irrigation and other agricultural projects. This is probably the reason farmers tend to disregard the frequent advice of irrigation authorities and experiment stations to move away from their regional "monoculture," whether it be cotton in northern Peru, rice in Thailand, or oranges in Sicily. By sticking by and large to the reliable cash crop, irrigation farmers forego perhaps the possibility of a more brilliant economic result, but considering the number of production problems they have to solve on newly irrigated land, they are probably justified in seeking to minimize demand uncertainty, at least during the first few years.

A second observation relates to the applicability of the R&D strategy to development project design. This vast subject can be explored here only quite fragmentarily.

The possibilities of considering multiple and parallel approaches aiming at reducing uncertainty before plunging for the one "best" approach, it will be objected, are strictly limited in most conventional projects. It is true that the intermediate stage of prototype production that lends itself particularly well to the idea of parallel approaches does not usually exist in development projects. Nevertheless, careful canvassing will uncover many areas where the habit of deciding in advance in favor of the one best way can be advantageously replaced by a more experimental approach allowing for some sequential decision making.

In irrigation projects, for example, the authorities frequently do not have reliable information about the most desirable cropping pattern. In this case, they have the perfectly respectable alternative of recommending a variety of such patterns. As it often takes many years for irrigation projects to become fully utilized, the pioneer water users are in effect buying information and reducing uncertainty for the latecomers. This relationship may well be and is in fact occasionally formalized, for example by free distribution of seed and fertilizer to the pioneers, particularly if they agree to take part in experimental plantings.

Similarly, when there is considerable uncertainty about the direction in which road traffic and new settlements will develop, it may be possible to build several cheap roads in lieu of a single expensive one and to wait for cues from the ensuing traffic to decide which one should be improved and perhaps paved.[28] The very unequal success of the various roads built in the course of highway construction programs—those of the Guayas committee are a good example—argues strongly for such a course. It seems that the art of estimating future road traffic on new roads is still quite undeveloped; hence the idea of breaking the decision-making mechanism down into two stages, with the first designed to reduce uncertainties and to buy information through multiple approaches, should have considerable appeal. It may be noted that the R&D strategy may to some extent be followed in planning roads, which can be built to very low standards, but hardly at all in planning railways—another important source of superiority of roads over railways.[29]

An excellent example of the project managers' stumbling, as it were, on the virtues of multiple approaches is provided by the Uruguayan pasture improvement project. Originally the replacing of the country's natural grasslands by artificial pastures had been conceived as a slow and costly process of ploughing up the fields and sowing a scientific mixture of new grasses and legumes. But little by little other methods were developed, such as the introduction into the existing grass cover of legume seeds through the seed sodder or of pelletized seeds

28. This is no more than a variant of the well-known idea of staged construction whose pros and cons are briefly discussed in Gary Fromm, "Design of the Transport Sector," in Gary Fromm (ed.), *Transport Investment and Economic Development* (Brookings Institution, 1965), pp. 102–03.

29. We are touching here on an important characteristic of projects— latitude in substituting quantity for quality—which is discussed in Chap. 3.

and fertilizers through spraying from airplanes. Individual landowners also experimented successfully with mere application of phosphatic fertilizer which gave vigor to the native clover and other legumes. In effect, therefore, the Uruguayan program adopted multiple approaches; and it is likely that each approach will continue to have its devotees as the usefulness of each depends on the type of terrain, the kind of management, and the amount of capital that are available.

The third observation on the mitigation of uncertainty takes as its starting point our findings on the possible trade-offs between uncertainties. We showed that by aiming at a reduction of demand uncertainty through the balanced-growth technique, one may well increase supply uncertainties because of the resulting impossibility of applying the R&D strategy. Surveying the argument in this chapter, it appears that this trade-off or seesaw relationship holds also for other pairs of uncertainties. For example, a decrease in financial uncertainty may stimulate administrative uncertainty as the securely financed project becomes more attractive to parasitic appetites and is under less pressure to put up a good performance.[30] The absence of technological complexity and uncertainty may make it similarly difficult to hold administrative uncertainty at bay.[31] The attempt to eliminate totally one particular kind of uncertainty may therefore not only be futile, but counterproductive.

The preceding statements can of course be turned around and will thereby acquire a more activist and hopeful ring: it will often be possible to mitigate some uncertainty, judged excessive or particularly obnoxious, by increasing another one.

As a result of this seesaw relationship between uncertainties, it is clear that project planners should think in terms of an

30. See p. 58.
31. See pp. 53–54.

optimal mix or constellation of the various uncertainties. Besides, even if eradication of uncertainty were possible, it would not be desirable. For the dangers that threaten when uncertainty is high usually have a counterpart in the correspondingly high payoff that accrues if they are overcome. Some of the most successful projects we have come across are those that have experienced substantial uncertainties and difficulties. Thus, optimal rather than minimal uncertainty or difficulty is the appropriate as well as the only feasible goal. We shall have more to say on this subject in Chapter 4.

CHAPTER THREE

Latitudes and Disciplines

THE PRECEDING CHAPTER may have given the impression that the behavior of projects is primarily a matter of meeting and coming to grips with a series of problems that arise in the process of setting up an organization, constructing capital facilities, producing outputs, and finding a market for them. In this view, a project's trajectory would be largely determined by forces impinging upon it from the outside, with the project planners and operators reacting more or less successfully to events beyond their control and frequently unforeseen by them. We have attempted to show which characteristics make projects specially vulnerable or resilient, as the case may be, to such buffeting by outside forces.

If, however, we are interested in understanding the different modes of project behavior, it is not sufficient to focus upon events that occur independently of and typically against the will of the project planners and operators; for the latter do have a certain freedom in charting the course of their projects, and the extent and use of this freedom will obviously be another important determinant of project behavior. I propose to designate by the term "latitude" this characteristic of a project (or task) that permits the project planner and operator to mold it, or to let it slip, in one direction or another, regardless of outside occurrences. Some projects are so structured that latitude is severely restricted or completely absent: in these cases I shall speak of lack of latitude or, positively, of the presence of "discipline" imparted by the project.

To focus on the concepts of latitude and discipline yields a special way of looking at the project decision, the project design, the choice of techniques, and similar topics that have already received considerable attention in the literature. Instead of looking at these decisions from the point of view of the "objective" analyst and his optimizing techniques, our inquiry shall deal with the propensities and pressures to which the decision makers themselves are subject. Special attention can thus be given to systematic departures of project execution from project design and, in line with our principal concern, to significant differences in this respect from one kind of project to the other. We can then examine ways and means of preventing or minimizing such departures or, alternatively, explore the rationality of systematic "misbehavior" of projects. In this indirect fashion, we may even hope to make some contribution to the science of project analysis and design.

Spatial or Locational Latitude

We begin our inquiry into latitude with the basic categories of space and time. Considering space first, one perceives a wide variation in the discipline project planners, builders, and operators are subject to in selecting a particular site for the project. We may borrow here from industrial location theory the distinction between site-bound and non-site-bound or "footloose" investments, extending it to the area of public investments with which we are primarily concerned. Site-bound investments consist most typically of the exploitation of some natural resource, such as a natural harbor or a natural damsite on a river, which is to be utilized for flood control, generation of hydropower, and/or irrigation; or of a particularly select location for a bridge, a canal, or a tunnel.

Irrigation projects themselves are not wholly site-bound, for within an irrigable area there is considerable room for variation in the design and extent of the canal network; they are clearly far more site-bound, however, than other projects of agricultural improvement that can be started virtually anywhere on a country's farmlands. In comparison to ports and hydropower installations, the location of highways, railways, and coal-burning thermal plants is not rigidly determined even though the nearby availability of aggregates and of coal and water, respectively, as well as other nature-given factors still plays an important role in the location decision for such projects.

Finally, there are many projects such as schools and hospitals whose location is wholly market-oriented; in other words, their location is not precisely imposed by some quirk or gift of nature, but more vaguely made desirable by the community's need for the service that is to be provided.

The effects of these locational characteristics on project behavior can be subdivided into effects (a) on the likelihood of the decision to go ahead with the project and on the speed with which the decision is taken, (b) on its probable quality, and (c) on the permanence and irreversibility of the decision.

There is little doubt that, in terms of decision making, strongly site-bound investment projects have an intrinsic advantage over projects of similar size and rate of return whose location is determined only in very general terms. This is best illustrated by investment choices within the same sector; in electric power, opportunities for hydro development are likely to be accorded some preference over alternative thermal installations; and in agriculture, irrigation projects will win more favors than general agricultural improvement projects.

Decision making is likely to be biased in favor of the site-bound investment simply because the case for it is straightforward and convincing to public opinion. The search for the country's comparative advantage and the quest for its identity both demand that a specific gift of nature be fully developed and utilized. The argument that a "free" natural resource is there waiting to be harnessed exerts a continuing attraction on engineers, politicians, and the public.[1] Hence the site-bound investment will usually have a somewhat irrational edge over non-site-bound projects serving the same sector. Moreover, the latter will labor under a handicap of their own which increases the edge of the former: the very fact that the location of non-site-bound investments is not imposed will often delay the investment decision. Location is an important component of that decision and it will be fought over, sometimes at length, by contending interests.

The preceding argument suffers from one unrealistic *ceteris paribus*: the bias in favor of the site-bound investment depended upon a choice between two investments of similar size. Ordinarily, however, the kind of site-bound investment we have been describing is likely to be much larger as well as less divisible than the typical non-site-bound investment, and this fact gives the latter a considerable edge at an early stage of development simply because the country's major site-bound investments are not yet feasible from the point of view of either resources or markets. The purpose of our *ceteris paribus* was to discern some typical traits of site-bound as opposed to non-site-bound projects; and it is already becoming clear that characteristic differences between the two kinds of projects affect not only the promptness of the investment decision, but the whole Gestalt of the decision-making process: In the case of site-bound (or should we say site-centered or site-attracted?) investments, the decision is more likely to be an emotional plunge, frequently accompanied by patriotic fervor and nationalist élan, either with no examination whatever of non-site-

1. Judith D. Tendler, "Technology and Economic Development: The Case of Hydro vs. Thermal Power," *Political Science Quarterly*, Vol. 80 (June 1965), pp. 236–53.

bound alternatives or with little serious competition from them. For non-site-bound investments, on the other hand, the decision-making process will be slower, marked by wrangles of opposing interest groups, but perhaps also by a rational examination of the alternatives.

Because the decision-making process is more laborious for non-site-bound investments, their proponents will sometimes attempt to disguise them as site-centered investments: For example, the highways radiating from Brasilia are essentially roads designed to open up Brazil's interior provinces for settlement and agricultural development; but the fact that they could be presented as roads linking the new capital to various existing centers (Belo Horizonte, Belém, Fortaleza, etc.) gave the case for such roads a new persuasiveness and urgency.[2]

The preceding characterization has a bearing on the quality of the investment decision for site-bound and non-site-bound investments. What has been said would seem to imply that site-bound projects have a power of seduction that makes a mediocre or dubious, if rapid, decision more likely than in the case of non-site-bound projects. Examples of such decisions are certainly easy to find, from the Owen Falls hydroelectric station in Uganda to Colombia's steel mill whose location at Paz de Rio was imposed by the nearby iron ore, coal, and limestone deposits. The site-bound investment is the prime candidate for the white elephant.

But the non-site-bound investment is by no means free of the risks of poor decision making, quite apart from the fact that it is exposed to the hazard of non-decision making. Whereas the site-bound project is often sponsored by the apex

2. The history of Brasilia itself illustrates the procrastination non-site-bound investments are prone to: the project goes back at least to 1890 when the constitution of the newly founded republic proclaimed the resolve to build a new capital "in the interior."

of the political structure, pressures and appetites for footloose projects are likely to come from all sections of the country. Hence, in comparison to site-bound investments, the dangers of fragmentation, political favoritism, inadequate funding, and poor engineering loom large in non-site-bound investments.

In countries like Brazil where the passion for development makes for much public airing of contrasting experiences with different kinds of projects, one can find on occasion incisive comments on these matters. In 1953 a bill setting up a Federal Electrification Fund was introduced in the Congress with the proviso that 60 percent of the revenue from the proposed electric power tax be distributed automatically to the states. This clause was criticized by some deputies on the following grounds: "The highway fund lends itself to this parcelling out of tax revenue into many handfuls so that, when the allotment is small, small too will be the road. In electric power, however, the situation is quite different. Electrification requires large plants—or at least plants of a certain size—constructed not wherever one fancies, but only where it is practicable to build them: where there is water, that is, and where that water falls."[3]

In the same vein, here is a fine example, from Nigeria, of what may happen to non-site-bound projects: "One of the most ironic illustrations of political communalism was seen in the siting of the national secondary schools that were intended to foster political integration. The three ministers who decided their location came from Sokoto, Warri and Afikpo: the schools were allocated to Sokoto, Warri and Afikpo."[4]

3. Câmara dos Deputados, Projeto No. 3204-c (Rio de Janeiro: Imprensa Nacional, 1953), p. 82.
4. J. O'Connell, "The Political Class and Economic Growth," *The Nigerian Journal of Economic and Social Studies*, Vol. 8 (November 1966), p. 137.

If we wish to look at the brighter side of things, we note that site-bound investments teach a country to take large-scale investment decisions, whereas non-site-bound investment can become a school for constructive political compromise and for rational choice among alternatives. By their nature, non-site-bound investments are usually considered and decided jointly or serially, and a whole group of them will normally be built and operated by one administrative agency (highway department, ministry of telecommunications or of education). They thus invite the formulation of *sector* programs while the site-bound investment is usually examined and decided in isolation; it is the mainstay of the "project approach" at least until it is built and in operation; thereafter, the agency responsible for it may well evolve into one that will take an interest in programs for the whole sector in which it is active, as a result of its experience and in order to extend its sphere of activity (the Lempa River Hydroelectric Commission of El Salvador is a good illustration of this tendency).

The autonomous agency device is used frequently for both site-bound and non-site-bound projects, but the results achieved and the record established by these agencies reflect the difference in the structure of these two kinds of projects. The agencies in charge of developing and operating a site-bound project or unified set of such projects have usually been fairly successful in charting their course and in pursuing their task, and have suffered little "political" intervention and interference. In fact, it is here that we encounter the major triumphs of the autonomous agency device. As examples we may cite not only El Salvador's Lempa River Hydroelectric Commission, but the Uganda Electricity Board which, in spite of being saddled with what was for many years a "white elephant," has always put in a highly creditable performance in the technical and administrative fields. Many similar examples could be cited from projects outside our sample. Agencies set up to develop a site-bound project are invested with the authority that comes with developing a national resource; whatever opposition there was to the undertaking has been vanquished with the decision to undertake the project and there is little expectation that the agency can be deflected from its uniquely laid out path. On the other hand, agencies administering footloose projects exhibit a far greater unevenness in performance; "insulation from politics" is unlikely to work here because too many decisions with wide-ranging political effects or implications must continuously be made; hence the work of the agency must somehow be made part of the political process and an attempt at "insulation" will be unsuccessful or may even weaken the agency's ability to perform its task properly. Among our projects, the Damodar Valley Authority supplies us with a particularly good illustration of this point, for as long as it stuck to site-bound investments—dams and connected hydro-plants—it was nicely "left alone," but it got into considerable political trouble with the states of West Bengal and Bihar over the siting of the comparatively footloose thermoelectric installations for the region.

Finally, the possibility of changing substantially the location of a project once it has been started, or of even going back entirely on the investment decision, differs sharply between site-bound and "footloose" projects. The likelihood of such decision-reversals is more extensive with footloose projects almost by definition. The decision on where to build a footloose project such as a road, a school, or even a thermal plant is likely to be more debated and is exposed to many more shifts than a decision on damming a river or on turning a natural harbor into a port. Hence the opponents of a non-site-bound project are likely to disarm much later and once they have given up, their place may well be taken by others who hope to influence and to modify the precise location of the project in one way or another.

Development Projects Observed

Even when it has been decided that a road will be built between two points, pressures can be exerted for layout changes, and once again project managers wishing to resist such pressures will attempt to make their project look as site-bound as possible: In Ecuador, for example, the Guayas highway committee, which was often subjected to considerable pressures by local landowners, decided during one period to build first just the bridges so that a road would in effect be divided into numerous segments that would be relatively short and far less "movable" than the total road layout. In this way the committee in effect tied its own hands, made sure that it could not be tempted, and so notified any would-be tempter.[5]

A similar reaction to pressures for decision changes was encountered in the San Lorenzo irrigation project in Peru: Here very strong pressures have continuously been exerted on the irrigation authority to abandon its plan to irrigate a certain desertic and sandy area known as Parkinsonia, whose conversion into farmland requires a heavy initial expenditure of both water and labor; these pressures originated primarily from downstream landowners who feared and disliked the San Lorenzo project in general for various reasons (see Chapter 2) but who concentrated their attack on the Parkinsonia area because it made a good target given its heavy need ("waste") for water. The contested area is located at the far end of the network of irrigation canals which, in the normal course of gradual development of the irrigation project, would have been tackled last. Had its development been deferred, the eventual fate of the area would have long remained uncertain and it is even conceivable that an anti-Parkinsonia coalition would have been formed between the plantation owners downstream and the al-

---

5. We have here a good example of the "power to bind oneself," which, as Thomas Schelling has shown, is a principal ingredient of bargaining power. See *The Strategy of Conflict* (Harvard University Press, 1960), pp. 22 ff.

ready established irrigation farmers, on the always plausible ground that more water for Y means less water for X. Faced with this situation, and imbued as it was with a sense of mission to develop the whole area entrusted to it, the irrigation authority decided to jump over several square miles of intervening territory and to develop the Parkinsonia area first instead of last, starting to boot with its outer rim. In this way the boundaries of the irrigation project area were clearly defined and the project became at once far more "site-bound" than it had been before.

Temporal Discipline in Construction

Applied to time, the concept of discipline, or lack of latitude, yields the category of the "time-bound" or, better perhaps, "time-schedule-bound" project which contrasts with the project where there is considerable latitude with respect to both progress of construction and the start of operation.

Like strictly site-bound projects, strictly time-schedule-bound ones tend to be limited to relatively few types, with nature once again providing the discipline, this time by wielding the baton rather than by pointing imperiously to a choice spot. Everyone is familiar with the rhythm that the periodicity of nature imposes on recurrent types of human activity and particularly on agricultural production. The disciplines it imposes on investment activity have been less noted—perhaps because they are less notable. Nevertheless, because they are very strong disciplines, they are a useful starting point for our discussion.

Engineers are fully aware that nature can be an important and highly useful spur in hurrying a construction project to completion or in keeping to a time table. The coming of winter in the temperate zone (or, lately, of the "long, hot summer" in the United States) and of the rainy season or the

monsoon in the tropics are of course the principal and most
powerful allies of those who are interested in pushing a project
along and in fighting ever-present inertia and delays as well as
diversion of men and equipment to other jobs.

These natural disciplines are actually compelling in quite
different ways and degrees. The rainy season may slow construction or it may completely halt it. In some cases, the progress of the work will be set back just for the duration of the
rains, but in others the penalty for delay is bigger: failure to
complete an irrigation dam before the rains come will often
mean that actual irrigation operations are delayed by a full
year since the needed waters can then be impounded only
during the next rainy season. But the penalty imposed and,
hence, the compulsion exerted by nature are strongest when
failure to complete the job by a certain date means that much
or all of the work already accomplished is destroyed, swept
away or otherwise lost. Such a situation exists when a dam
must be built up high enough to hold back the river once it
is monsoon-swollen; and this compulsion to build the dam up
to a certain height during a single dry season is usually a consequence of designing for economy reasons a low-capacity
diversion channel that can contain the river flow during the
dry, but not during the wet, season.

Both the Tilaya and the Maithon dams of the Damodar
Valley Corporation were built under this discipline. The extraordinary responsibility that rests in this situation on the
project managers and the sense of drama, mission, and eventually achievement that it communicates to all participants have
been vividly conveyed by Henry C. Hart:

On the morning of 8 June 1953, Mr. A. M. Komora, the chief
engineer, took me to the edge of the freshly cut channel into
which the D.V.C. was going to move the Barakar River. The
channel was 350 feet wide; it had been cut through clay and
boulders deep into the grey bedrock to river-bed level. Upstream,

it stopped just short of the Barakar's waters. The monsoon when it came, would quickly raise the river enough to spill over the unexcavated end and rush down the artificial channel until it re-entered the natural riverbed, almost a mile downstream. . . .

Beyond the still dry diversion channel, and the dammed river, ran yet a third channel. This one was out of sight, an 1100-foot tunnel. . . . It was now carrying the entire dry-weather flow of the Barakar.

That panorama told at a glance how daring, and how crucial, was the season's target for Maithon Dam. In 1952, a contracting firm had driven the tunnel through the hills on the opposite bank in time to divert the low waters of the Barakar. This year, the D.V.C. had to do two things at once: to build up the earthen dam across the river-bed high enough and strong enough to block the biggest monsoon floods; and to get the diversion trench deep enough so that, with the tunnel's help, those floods could find their way safely around the flank of the earthen dam. In short, they were trying to move a good-sized river out of its bed and permanently to dam that bed, in eight months of a single working season. It was, indeed, a target beyond Old India's reach.

. . . D.V.C. had spent two painful years finding the men who could meet deadlines—and weeding out those who could not.[6]

Another one of our projects provides a different illustration of the importance of meeting nature's deadlines. When I visited Ecuador, maintenance and reconstruction of the road from Guayaquil to Quevedo were being pushed with considerable energy: for, so I was told, if the road were not substantially improved by the time of the rainy season, the heavy banana traffic together with the rains could easily bring about a catastrophe for Ecuador's economy—inability to evacuate a good part of the banana crop as large sections of the road became impassable.

Although it is difficult to give many examples, pressure toward prompt prosecution and completion of a construction job is probably often generated by the conjunction of a certain

6. *New India's Rivers* (Calcutta: Orient Longmans, 1956), pp. 81–83.

technology with the mere passing of time. This is the case when phase one of a job should be followed rapidly by phase two because otherwise "the elements" would inflict considerable damage on the results of phase one. One case in point here is the concrete lining of irrigation canals that must follow rapidly upon the earth-moving operations because rains, winds, and wandering animals will play havoc with purely earthen structures left alone for long. A more significant illustration is the impulse toward soil conservation and erosion control that comes with the completion of a dam and the filling up of a reservoir behind it: the danger that the completed reservoirs of the Damodar Valley will silt up in a few years as a result of erosion has been responsible for some of the best Indian work in soil conservation.

Discipline, due to strong cues of these kinds from nature, is more unambiguously valuable in a developing country when it helps to set up a firm time schedule than when it merely points to a particular location. Once the investment decision, good or bad, is made, any mechanism that promotes speed of construction and adherence to a time schedule will be greatly welcome. Moreover, in the cases first cited, nature performs a training function as well: its cues and compulsions will teach the operators to meet deadlines and, provided they have learned and "internalized" nature's lesson, these same operators may then be both better able and more motivated to keep to a time schedule in other tasks where nature does not collaborate to the same extent or perhaps at all.

If nature fails to supply boundedness, everything does not necessarily depend on whether the project managers and their staff are able and willing to set themselves deadlines and to meet them. Deadlines are being set for them from the outside not only by nature, but by contractual arrangements as when fines are incurred by contractors if they do not finish the job by a certain time; this is an important reason why it is sometimes found advisable to let contractors handle certain jobs that could be done departmentally.

Another kind of pressure toward promptness could come from the would-be users of the to-be-constructed facility. Such users presumably have a strong economic interest in rapid completion and will act or cause others to act accordingly. When there is a power shortage, for example, there will be very strong pressures on a power company to push ahead with construction of new generating capacity and to be ready with a transmission and distribution network once a new generating station is completed. Under conditions of power shortage, the prospective completion date of the generating station thus can set a deadline as effective for the transmission and distribution system as that set up by the monsoon for dam or road construction.[7]

With some types of projects, it is possible for well informed and eager would-be users of the new facility to "jump the gun," to act and invest as though the facility were already available: caught short they will then have a considerable stake in rapid completion and can be relied on to exert pressures in this direction unless they either go broke immediately or make more or less satisfactory "temporary" arrangements that reduce the urgency of their need. The latter situation applies to industrialists who locate in an area where new power supplies were to become available but are delayed, and who are thereby forced to install their own diesel generators. Sometimes such "premature" customers could be lost for good, as in the case of the groundnut crushing mill that located at Maiduguri (northeastern Nigeria) in anticipation of the promised railroad link, but made satisfactory arrangements for having its oil and

7. For a detailed account of such situations in Brazil, see Judith D. Tendler, *The Rise of Public Power in Brazil* (to be published in 1968 by Harvard University Press), Chap. 7.

groundnut cake carried to the ports in trucks when various technical and administrative difficulties held up first the completion of the link and then a half-mile spur from Maiduguri station to the mill.

With other projects, alternatives such as diesel generators or trucks are less available: this was the case of the Ecuadoran farmer-entrepreneurs who, during the banana boom of the fifties, started to grow bananas in areas that were due to be penetrated by a road, but that lacked any satisfactory alternative means of evacuation for the bulky fruit. Similarly, in certain areas of the Catania irrigation project in Sicily, citrus fruit growers would terrace the land, plant orange trees, and then water them by laboriously bringing in water from rivers or wells as soon as it became known that these areas were to be irrigated. In terms of concepts used in my *Strategy of Economic Development*, we have here a good example of directly productive activities (DPA) getting just a little ahead of social overhead capital (SOC), in fact so little that they cannot activate the decision to invest in social overhead capital since this decision has already been made and is in fact responsible for the directly productive activities (planting of banana or orange trees); but those activities (DPA) still make a not unimportant contribution by goading the lagging road or irrigation project (SOC) to rapid completion.

When inertia or opposing interests slow the pace of a project's construction and organization, the project authorities will sometimes foment this kind of pressure from the outside, on the part of the project's prospective users; by thus bringing highly visible pressure on themselves they can be more convincing in making their case for the financial, legal, or other support they are being denied. The directors of the San Lorenzo irrigation scheme engaged fairly successfully in just this tactic: they used the presence and the squatting of local goatherds and landless farmers (*precaristas*) in the to-be-irrigated area as an important argument in lobbying for the project with the Lima authorities who at times were not too keen about getting on with the scheme.

When all else fails there remains of course a well-known device for reducing temporal latitude: the political deadline for the completion and inauguration of a project. Projects that lend themselves to being inaugurated with great pomp not only have a notoriously privileged position in competing for public funds; once approved in principle, they are likely to be pushed along somewhat more energetically if they must be ready to start operations on a certain day when the president or minister will cut the ribbon. Naturally, unlike the onset of the rainy season, this day can be postponed time and again so that the discipline of a political deadline is less strict than that of nature. Still, a request for postponement means loss of prestige and may mean loss of a job for the project director. Moreover, an effort can be made to imitate nature more closely and to render the deadline unmovable by announcing in advance that a project will be inaugurated on a highly symbolic date, such as the national holiday. Similarly, when the highest political authority has a limited term in office and is intent on being given credit for a project, the deadline is not indefinitely postponable—a considerable effort will then be made to get the project completed and inaugurated before the term of the president expires. And this effort will be even greater when the outgoing president suspects that his successor will discontinue or undo "his" project much as the monsoon-swollen river destroys the half-completed earthen dam. The most famous recent case of this "president-bound" type of project is the rushing to completion and the inauguration of Brasilia in early 1960 by President Kubitschek.[8] The counterpart to this situa-

8. An earlier instance of this kind of project in Brazil which, however, was not finished in time and was then duly abandoned by the next president is retold in *Journeys Toward Progress*, pp. 32–34.

tion is the new regime that loses interest in, or is even actively hostile to, a project that was started under the predecessor. Many of the difficulties of the San Lorenzo irrigation scheme must be traced to the fact that it was started but not completed under the Odría regime and had during that time been violently attacked by Pedro Beltrán, who became Peru's powerful prime minister under Odría's successor Manuel Prado. Nevertheless, regularity of presidential succession may have— among other far more important virtues—the advantage that it motivates each succeeding president to select some specific programs and projects he wishes associated with his name and then to push them through to completion during his term of office.

In the preceding discussion of temporal latitude, it has been our implicit assumption that speed in construction and in assuring utilization is desirable, that any falling behind schedule or delay in project completion is essentially due to weaknesses in organization and motivation that should be overcome, and that, outside perhaps of the violence that is inflicted on attitudes and ingrained habit, there is essentially no cost involved in forcing the pace through the various devices that have been surveyed. This assumption must now be briefly questioned.

In almost any project, speedup may involve extra monetary costs through payment of overtime and similar factors. In some categories of projects, moreover, speedup is likely to entail another kind of cost: shoddiness in construction. Speed may be bought at the expense of quality, of throwing overboard strict adherence to specifications; this is likely to happen when there is a great deal of latitude in the quality of construction—a topic that will be discussed shortly. It should be stated right away, however, that as soon as the possibility of incurring this kind of cost is realized, it becomes clear that there can be limits to the desirability of time-schedule-boundedness and of speedup mechanisms during construction.

Temporal Discipline from Construction to Operation

The discussion of temporal latitude and of spurs to time-schedule discipline has dealt exclusively thus far with the various stages of the construction process. Actually it would be most desirable to have such a spur also for the next stages, namely the passage from the end of construction to the beginning of operation and from there to capacity operation. Slowness (sometimes outright nonoccurrence) of this passage represents, on the whole, an even greater danger to the success of projects than slowness of construction. Unfortunately, mechanisms that would exert pressure toward ensuring and speeding up this passage are not easy to come by. In the first place, the kinds of disciplines so far discussed act primarily on the motivations of the project personnel; the operation of the completed facility, unlike its construction, does not depend solely or principally on the project managers or sponsors, but on outside demand for the project's outputs. Secondly, in the case of revenue-producing projects, the sponsors already have the strongest conceivable incentive to get the completed project fully utilized as quickly as possible; but with non-revenue-producing projects, such as roads, they have a negligible or zero interest in utilization which it may be extraordinarily difficult to raise to a significant level.[9]

In any event, our search for spurs to promptness beyond the construction stage has been rather unsuccessful. Financial in-

9. The incentive that springs from earning revenue should operate also in the construction phase—the sooner a project gets completed, the sooner will revenue begin to be earned; nevertheless, the various devices that have been described have been found very useful, since these more proximate pressures supplement and reinforce the income-earning motive which may be a bit weak when operation still lies far in the future, particularly in the case of publicly operated facilities in the fields of electric power and irrigation; in the case of non-revenue-producing projects, the presence of these devices is of course even more welcome.

centives apart, the latitude project managers have in delaying the start of operations after construction is completed is singularly wide. If nonuse of a completed facility had a physically ruinous effect on that facility, we would have something corresponding to the monsoon-generated discipline in dam construction. But no such situation can be discovered, except for the natural deterioration that comes with nonuse and that is a small matter next to the loss of revenue. One important additional penalty for nonuse after construction, however, is loss of prestige for all those connected with the project. The fear of such a loss may act as a spur on the managers to do everything in their power to find customers for the goods and services they have to supply. We must therefore inquire which types of projects will be equipped with this particular spur.

In order to be able to gain or lose prestige for its sponsors, a project's success or failure must be *visible*, its utilization, or the lack of it, must be obvious, clear-cut, measurable. Since railways operate rolling stock and publish traffic statistics, lack of utilization is far more visible for them than for roads. Again, when there is a fairly clear notion of the capacity of the facility, failure becomes quantifiable and hence also more visible: in irrigation projects, for example, statistics as to the percentage of the irrigable area that is actually irrigated are usually available and often point an accusing finger at the irrigation authorities; no such data are publicly available on a periodic basis for roads.

To a considerable extent, the projects where failure or success is visible overlap with the revenue-producing projects, and the revenue-making motive is bolstered in these cases by the desire to avoid prestige loss. But among the projects that are relieved of the obligation to earn revenue, some, like highways or schools, are also far freer of the fear of prestige loss than others, like irrigation projects.[10] And this difference may help explain the fact that even when there is no charge for water, irrigation authorities often make considerable efforts to improve the degree of water utilization, by building additional field channels and by supplying technical and financial assistance to farmers, while highway or school authorities are not usually known to engage in follow-up activities designed to increase utilization of the roadbed or of their graduates, respectively. The argument suggests that to make project authorities more sensitive to the risks of prestige loss and hence more interested in exploring ways of encouraging utilization, it may be helpful to increase visibility, for example, through the production and periodic publication of statistical and other information on the degree of utilization of the project's capacity or output.[11]

In some projects, delay in utilization carries one further danger that should, if realized, act as a spur to managers: the project, rather than lose money or prestige, will lose its *soul*; its capacity is eventually utilized, but for purposes alien to its original mission.

Two examples from our sample will help explain this point. In the San Lorenzo irrigation scheme the storage dam and main canal system that diverted some of the water of the Quiroz River toward the San Lorenzo plateau and from there into the Piura were ready long before any irrigation in the San

10. The argument applies strictly only to irrigation projects that do not charge for water, like those in Thailand and several in India. In the case of schools we are referring not to lack of utilization of the schools themselves, but to the much more common failure on the part of society properly to utilize their output, that is, the graduates.

11. Under the spur of competition, private schools in the United States supply this kind of information when they tell the parents of their prospective customers which percentage of their graduates they are able to place in the better colleges.

Lorenzo area was brought underway. During the years that the waters were not used for their original purpose, they were channeled directly to the Lower Piura Valley to be used there by the established cotton plantations whose productive acreage consequently increased considerably. While the dammed up waters were thus turned to very good account, specially from the point of view of the Lower Piura plantation owners who received them free, this success went at the expense of the original objective of establishing agricultural activities in a new area. The contrast between actual achievement and proclaimed objective became even sharper when the objective was modified to include the establishment of family-size farms in the San Lorenzo area and the settlement of landless and poor farmers. In theory (and in law), the irrigation scheme was to open up new land for agricultural production, but to do this in such a way as to introduce a new pattern of landholding. In effect, the scheme served for a number of years exclusively to increase the area under the control of the plantation owners and, in the process, the rich became richer even though some additional employment was no doubt created and foreign exchange was earned by the cotton exports. It took a great deal of reform-minded energy to get the project back on its intended track against the strong and resourceful opposition of its unintended beneficiaries.

A rather similar situation arose in Uganda whose Electricity Board had brought the Owen Falls Hydroelectric Station into being, only to find that most of its generating capacity was idle for lack of power consumers. One of the fundamental purposes of the power station had been to make possible an important industrial center in Uganda that would, in the interests of regional balance and harmony in Britain's East African territories, counteract the industrial predominance of Nairobi, Kenya's capital. But when the Uganda Electricity Board found itself with all that installed power on its hands, one obvious step toward financial relief was to build a transmission line to Kenya and sell in that comparatively power-hungry market a substantial block of domestically unsalable power. This step was taken in 1955, and the Owen Falls scheme thereby served to make more power available to Kenya, thus further increasing that country's attraction for new industry, in the sharpest possible contrast to the original mission of the project.

This "loss of soul" or of original purpose can apparently happen to projects that linger too long between completion and capacity operation. The projects that are prone to it are those whose services can be diverted away from the intended beneficiaries; and it may happen primarily when a project, as was the case in both Peru and Uganda, is meant to change a strongly entrenched social and economic structure by offering an advantage to a hitherto underprivileged group or region: frequently that structure is so strongly entrenched that in the end the project, in spite of all its good intentions, will further increase the advantages and fortunes of the privileged.

Latitude for Corruption

In examining, in the preceding sections of this chapter, the influence on project behavior of latitude with respect to space and time, I have been extending into new territory a concept I had related essentially to quality and quantity in my *Strategy of Economic Development*.[12] I now turn to amplify, but also to qualify, the concept in its original domain.

Briefly put, the original argument went as follows: underdeveloped countries are by definition poorly equipped with managerial and organizational talent; in newly established, highly protected industries the spur of competition is frequently missing; the labor force is often untrained and the

12. See Chap. 8, "Efficiency and Growth of the Individual Firm."

instinct of workmanship has not become "second nature." Hence, in those industrial tasks where there is wide latitude for poor performance, actual performance will gravitate toward the poor end of the scale. By the same token, where there is least latitude, or most discipline, performance will more nearly equal that of the older industrial countries. This consideration led to a search for characteristics of industrial processes—high penalty for nonmaintenance, machine-paced rather than labor-paced processes, process-centered rather than product-centered production, etc.—that through the reduction of latitude could be expected to induce respectable levels of quality and quantity performance.[13]

The argument related exclusively to production processes, to the *operation* of production facilities already in existence, and it seems to me to retain much of its validity when applied to the operation of the kind of investment projects under discussion here. In fact, I shall suggest now a new application of the earlier analysis. Let us introduce corruption as one of the components of poor performance in operation—more correctly perhaps, as one of the determining factors, because of its deleterious effect on general staff morale in an organization. In a society where corruption is rampant, we will therefore expect

13. These hypotheses have been largely confirmed by what few empirical tests have been conducted to date. See Carlos F. Diaz Alejandro, "Industrialization and Labor Productivity Differentials," *Review of Economics and Statistics*, Vol. 47 (May 1965), pp. 207–14; and Christopher Clague, *Economic Efficiency in Peru and the United States* (unpublished doctoral dissertation, Harvard University, 1966). In line with the general argument of my earlier book, the hypotheses implied a widespread propensity to tolerate "slack" and a corresponding failure to move to the "production frontier" unless special pressure or pacing mechanisms are brought into play or unless the technical characteristics of the production process simply rule out slack. Important empirical and theoretical foundations for these concepts have recently been provided by Harvey Leibenstein in his article, "Allocation Efficiency versus X-Efficiency," *American Economic Review*, Vol. 56 (June 1966), pp. 392–415.

projects that have a latitude for corruption to do worse than those with little or no such latitude. But are there any of the latter projects? Probably not in the construction phase, but in operation there is little possibility of corruption, for example, when operating expenses are low, when the services provided by the facility are given free of charge, and when its capacity is underutilized so that there is no problem of allocating the output among the prospective users. This is typically the case of highways. However much graft may have been involved in getting a highway built, and however graft-ridden the highway department, the efficiency of trucking operations is not going to suffer in consequence. The truckers are an entirely distinct group of operators; their morale is not likely to be affected even if they know that the building of the highway involved graft; moreover, short of harrassments by the highway police, the actual utilization of the highway does not offer room for "deals" between the users and the highway department.

With railways the situation is wholly different. Any irregularity and consequent lowering of staff morale that occurred in the construction phase (say, during the building of the Bornu extension in Nigeria) stays in the system and affects the efficiency of operations, for the same organization is responsible for both phases. Moreover, the operations phase is independently subject to the intrusion of corrupt practices, for example, in conjunction with the preferential allocation of freight cars during rush periods. Hence, any comparison of transport costs for rail and road that does not attempt to correct for likely differences in their levels of performance due to such factors will fail to do justice to the real advantages of road over rail transport in a corruption-ridden country.[14]

14. See Chap. 4 for a similar argument for countries affected by strong tribal conflicts.

A somewhat different example illustrating the same point comes from the field of electric power. Generation of power is a far less malpractice-prone activity than distribution: in distribution, special favors to larger consumers can be negotiated and some VIP bills may never be collected, whereas generation is a purely technical task, with power being sold in bulk at the substations to the company or companies in charge of the distribution network. Hence, in countries where the granting of personal favors by public officials is widely expected, requested, or paid for, public power companies may perform quite efficiently in the field of generation, but experience considerable difficulty in distribution. This is probably one reason why foreign *private* companies have survived longer in distribution than in generation; in El Salvador, I was told specifically that in a small country with an extensive and powerful *amigo* network, it may be unwise for a public power company to get involved in distribution, however successful it was in generation.[15]

A similar reluctance to shift from an activity where there is no latitude for corruption or extortion to one where considerable possibilities of this kind have long been exploited was encountered in the Volturno irrigation project in southern Italy. Here farmers were said to be reluctant to replace the traditional cereal and water buffalo economy of the area by utilizing the available irrigation waters to grow high-value garden crops such as tomatoes and other vegetables, for in doing so, they would come under the control of the powerfully entrenched "Camorra" (Naples' equivalent of Sicily's Mafia) which allegedly dominates the fruit and vegetable trade in and around Naples.

15. Public enterprise is drawn into, and is likely to be at its best, in generation—particularly hydro-generation—rather than in distribution, for several other reasons that are analyzed in Tendler, *The Rise of Public Power in Brazil*, passim.

These considerations can be made to yield a cautionary foot-note to the policy advice, frequently given by fiscal experts to public authorities in underdeveloped countries, to charge for services rendered whenever there exists a capacity to pay for them. While this is usually sound policy, one rarely realizes that charging for irrigation water, for example, could introduce latitude for corruption and malpractices into water distribution by the irrigation authorities and might thereby endanger whatever esprit de corps, morale, and public-serving attitudes it has been possible to instill in the personnel of the irrigation department. Thailand's Royal Irrigation Department has been quite successful in these respects, and this may be one element in the preference of Thai policy makers for the export tax on rice over the assessment of the rice farmer for irrigation water. The latter course is unambiguously more efficient only as long as the differential latitude for corruption of various tax- or revenue-levying arrangements is disregarded.

Our argument must not be interpreted to mean that corruption-prone or -ridden countries should eschew entirely all activities in which there is latitude for corruption or miscellaneous malpractices. In the first place, such a rule would condemn these countries to stagnation. Secondly, the only way in which a country can eventually learn how to deal with these problems is by facing them—this should of course be done at a time in the country's development and by an agency such that the odds against succumbing are tolerably high. An example of learning comes from Ethiopia: that country's Imperial Board of Telecommunications had no option but to face the problem of collecting telephone bills due from government agencies and VIP's. It was defeated at first: considerable arrears accumulated and could finally be "paid" only by offsetting them against a nominal dividend distribution by the board to the government; thereafter, however, a fairly impersonal and prompt collection system was set up and this success meant a veritable breakthrough for "universalist" values that also helped strengthen the morale of the board's own staff.

Latitude in Substituting Quantity for Quality

Up to this point, my earlier notions on latitude for poor performance have been extended and enriched. Now comes the time for the already announced qualifications. Turning to the construction, rather than operation, of projects, projects with no latitude for poor quality have the usual advantage that they are likely to be built in accordance with the rigid standards and specifications that they by definition require in order to function at all. Electric power stations, large dams, bridges, even railways belong in this category. It is also correct that when the penalty for nonadherence to established quality standards is milder than in the cases just named, some slippage is likely to occur so that the quality of such projects as roads, irrigation canals, buildings, etc. will typically leave something to be desired. But just as we noted that speeding up construction may have a cost in terms of quality, so we must now take into account the possibility that a sacrifice of quality may be compensated by more rapid construction of a given quantity or—and this comes to essentially the same thing—by an increase in quantity.

A very important example of substitutability between quantity and quality is furnished by education. In this sector, a given "plant" consisting of teaching staff, buildings, libraries, etc. can produce different output combinations, with the quantity of output (number of graduates per year) varying inversely with the number of years of schooling required—which number presumably has something to do with quality.

Among our projects, roads (in Ecuador) were the most important example of this substitutability. By skimping on the thickness of the base of a road, one can build a longer (and poorer quality) road than originally envisaged with the same input of materials, labor, and machines; it is here possible and not infrequently irresistible to substitute quantity for quality in construction while, in other kinds of projects, such a substitution is either technologically impossible or, when possible, unthinkable because of the risks involved.

A very similar substitution is that of new construction for maintenance. In road building this substitution is again possible, not only financially but physically: the same machinery, labor, and materials used for maintaining old roads (and irrigation ditches) can almost all be used just as well to build new mileage, whereas in electric power generation, for example, this substitution is technically impossible—one can't start building a new power plant with the lubricating oils or spare parts that serve to keep the machines in the old plant in good repair. Moreover, even if substitution were possible, it would again be unthinkable because of the narrow tolerance of electrical machinery.

Substitution of quantity for quality and of new construction for maintenance are essentially the same phenomenon: both result in a different quality-quantity mix of the system. As long as the sacrifice of quality is compensated by an increase in quantity, it is impossible a priori to condemn this substitution or the latitude in quality that makes it possible. Such latitude is unequivocally "bad" only when tampering with quality does not release resources that can be and are used to increase quantity—this is essentially the case of the industrial processes to which I addressed myself in my earlier book.

When tampering with quality results in larger quantity, we have a typical allocation problem that can be explored by conventional tools of analysis. At any one time, a country's highway authority has a certain amount of earth-moving and road-building machinery, materials, and labor which we may assume to have, for the sake of simplicity, just two kinds of outputs: undermaintained, low-quality road mileage and well maintained, high-quality mileage. If all the available inputs are used for the "production" of the former category, more mileage will be produced (say, a third more) than if only good roads are built and high standards of maintenance are observed. A transformation curve resulting from these assumptions is drawn in Figure 1. It shows the possible combinations of well maintained and undermaintained mileage that can be produced with the available resources, and it has been given the conventional convex shape on the assumption that some machinery, although usable for new construction, is better suited for maintenance, and vice versa. Which is the ideal "mix" from the country's point of view—that is, which point on the curve should be chosen—depends on the ratio of the social marginal productivity (SMP) of well maintained (m) to that of undermaintained (u) mileage. Ordinarily we have of course $SMP_m > SMP_u$ with the limiting case of equality that would occur in a country where existing mileage is grossly inadequate and where the economic opportunities any sort of new mileage would open up are very large. Here new mileage is everything and its quality is a wholly secondary consideration. This limiting case is shown by point P which is the point of tangency with a line parallel to MM' forming an angle of 45 degrees with the two axes. The point P is also and logically the combination that maximizes total mileage. It is clear that this is the limit to which any rational policy would go, for under no circumstances would one wish to substitute unmaintained for maintained mileage if the result is a loss in quantity as well as in quality; yet this is what happens on the PU segment of the transformation curve. The possible mixes lie therefore on the PM segment; for countries where the highway network is underdeveloped in relation to economic opportunities, the appropriate mix, shown as point L, is more likely to

FIGURE 1. *Combinations of Maintenance Standards for a Highway System.*

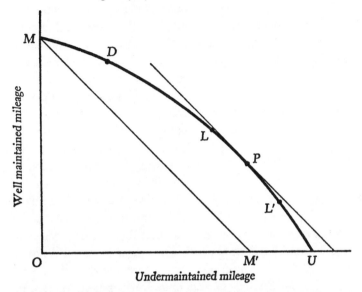

lie in the vicinity of *P*. In countries with a mature transportation system and with competing modes of transport, on the other hand, the social marginal productivity (*SMP*) of well maintained mileage is likely to exceed greatly that of unmaintained mileage: this relationship results in a price line that will be almost parallel to the horizontal axis, and such a line will touch the transformation curve at *M* or at a point close to *M*, such as *D*, indicating that the advanced country should build, comparatively, a quite small number of poorly maintained roads.

Different countries thus may require different "mixes" of maintained and undermaintained mileage; therefore, up to a certain point the neglect of maintenance or the poor quality of the roads so often noted in developing countries is not just negligence and inertia, but a rational adaptation to distinc-

tive requirements of the economy. Ideally this adaptation
should result from a conscious decision to build lower quality
roads and to adopt lower standards of maintenance than is the
rule in developed countries. But given the usual emulation by
the underdeveloped countries of the standards prevailing in
developed countries, economic rationality must often assert
itself by the underhanded diversion of equipment meant for
maintenance to new construction and by skimping on road
building materials in the interest of augmented mileage. In
Ecuador, such diversion and skimping took place in response
to pressures from local interests and also from newly established banana plantation owners who, as already mentioned,
would often plant a little ahead of the supply of transportation
services. Naturally, not every such diversion and skimping is
desirable; as a result of latitude with respect to quality, the
point L may well be overshot, so that the country reaches instead point L' or even U which is no longer economically justified.[16] Still, this would be a better outcome than if, as I assumed in my *Strategy of Economic Development*, there were
no compensation whatsoever for the decline in quality induced
by latitude. In that case all the mileage that could be built and
maintained in good condition with the resources in hand

16. A strong *unjustified* bias in favor of new construction and against
maintenance may exist for the following reasons: "the relatively high cost
of maintenance; the shortage of technical skills; the requirement for fore-
sight in terms of planned acquisition of equipment, training of personnel
and organization for the execution of maintenance; and the lack of realization of the real costs (direct and indirect) of not taking preventive or
restorative maintenance measures. Furthermore, the developing country
frequently finds it easier to obtain foreign loans for new construction than
to obtain increased taxes for maintenance." Gary Fromm, "Design of the
Transport Sector," in Gary Fromm (ed.), *Transport Investment and Economic Development* (Brookings Institution, 1965), p. 102. The un-
doubted presence of these causes of bias does not cancel the fact that a
part of the bias in favor of new construction may be justified for the reasons stated in the text.

would in fact be poorly built and undermaintained, without any gain in total mileage, so that the country's highway system would be represented by point M'.

The preceding remarks have a bearing on the institutional framework of highway construction and maintenance. Precisely in order to block the technically feasible substitution of new construction for maintenance, separate highway maintenance departments with substantial autonomy have been established in a number of countries, sometimes with active advice from international agencies. While these autonomous organizations can be useful in counteracting the excesses of substitution that may occasionally take place, our analysis suggests that they should probably not be so independent as to be impervious to pressures for substitution that may be wholly rational.

At the beginning of this section it was noted that education is another sector in which it is possible to substitute quantity for quality. The preceding argument is, in fact, almost entirely applicable to education, and so is the diagram if one substitutes, say, graduates with 12-year and 9-year schooling, respectively, for well and poorly maintained mileage as its coordinates. But one difference will be noted: whereas in roads the project managers occasionally tamper with the quality specifications either directly in the course of construction or through undermaintenance in order to achieve an increment in quantity, no such action to conform with the requirements of the economy appears to be available to the managers of the educational system of an underdeveloped country.

If the educational system has been set up, as it often is, with uneconomically high standards and overly long schooling periods in imitation of the advanced countries, there seems to be no other way in which rationality can assert itself than through outright educational reform. Yet, upon looking more

closely, one can detect an equivalent of the tampering with
specifications or neglect of maintenance typical of road construction: in education the substitution of quantity for quality
is performed not by the managers but by the *outputs* themselves—for they are animated beings endowed not only with a
soul, but with the ability to respond to market situations. A
large number of those who drop out of school do so presumably because the economy is as ready to absorb them with their
limited amount of schooling as it would be if they were to finish. As a result of the high dropout rate in the upper grades, a
larger number of students can be accommodated in the lower
grades than would otherwise be possible, and the educational
pyramid is flattened out. The dropouts thus make the educational system yield in effect an output whose quantity-quality
mix is quite different from the one for which the system was
designed. Like undermaintenance of highways, the high dropout rate characteristic of many less developed countries may to
some extent be justified by viewing it as an attempt to correct
the rigid and overambitious standards copied from foreign
models.[17]

In both highways and education, actual technological latitude in substituting quantity for quality is wider than conventional standards permit, and we have shown how, in response
to pressing demands from the environment, the conventional
limits can be and are being widened. The housing sector provides a particularly pronounced example of such an adaptation.
Here again, prevailing and traditional standards of the indus-

17. The above argument on the possible rationality of dropping out of
school is strictly limited to the case of overdesigned schooling systems; for
a more general (and much more dubious) argument, valid, that is, for any
country and based on "consumer sovereignty," see Burton A. Weisbrod,
"Preventing High School Dropouts," in Robert Dorfman (ed.), *Measur-
ing Benefits of Government Investments* (Brookings Institution, 1965),
p. 119.

try have prevented a full exploitation of the considerable quan-
tity-for-quality substitutions that are actually feasible. But as
the requirements of shelter for low-income immigrants have
dramatically increased in many cities, these substitutions have
been carried out directly, if chaotically, by those who needed
them, namely by the immigrants themselves. Through the
building up of *favelas, ranchos, barriadas,* and similar shanty
town settlements, these immigrants are in effect diverting the
capacity of the building materials industry toward a quantity-
quality mix that is socially more appropriate than the one that
would prevail without their initiative, while indicting, at the
same time, the building industry and public housing officials
for their failure to push through, in a more orderly manner,
such changes in the mix as are clearly in the public interest.[18]

Latitude in Substituting Private for Public Outlays

There is one further reason why latitude with respect to both
quality in construction and maintenance after construction is
not necessarily or wholly an evil, but may result in a roundabout assertion of economic rationality. Returning to roads
and looking at the matter from the point of view of the total
cost of providing transportation services in a mixed economy,
poorly built or poorly maintained roads represent a device for
reducing the portion of that cost defrayed by the public sector
and for increasing by the same token—that is, as a result of
the poor driving conditions—private outlays for tires, spare
parts, depreciation, drivers' salaries, etc. The poor quality of
the road means therefore that private outlays for transportation investment and current costs are forcibly substituted for

18. This view of shanty town settlements owes much to conversations
with Lisa Peattie and John C. Turner, of the M.I.T.-Harvard Joint Center
for Urban Studies.

public outlays in the total cost of the services provided to the economy.[19]

In effect, latitude for *quality* is here a particular "manifestation" of latitude for the *quantity* or share of the public sector's contribution that may exist in any production task undertaken jointly by the private and public sectors. This latitude again varies structurally from one category of public investment to another. For rail and air transport it is obviously much narrower than for roads: first of all, because the public sector is usually responsible also for the carriers; and even if the carriers are in private hands, as can be the case for airlines, the technical possibility for the (private) airlines to make up, by outlays of their own, for the public sector's default on a portion of its "normal" contribution—for example, for a landing strip of poor quality or in poor repair—is quite limited in comparison to the latitude for this sort of substitution in highways.

As already mentioned, this latitude takes various forms. In the case of highways, since private transporters do not usually build them, an attempt to minimize the public contribution manifests itself in the poor quality of the road network. When latitude for quality variation is narrow, as for example in electric power, it may be possible to get the private sector to assume responsibility for supplying part or all of a service elsewhere provided wholly by the public sector. Industrial firms in developing countries have often been obliged to supply a portion of their power requirements by installing generating plants of their own; sometimes, when the public utility provides base loads, these facilities will be used on a standby basis or to meet peak loads.

In irrigation projects, the respective responsibilities of the irrigation authorities and the farmers are often similarly ill

19. For some data, see R. B. Heflebower, "Characteristics of Transport Modes," in Fromm (ed.), *op. cit.*, pp. 52–54.

defined: the irrigation authorities usually expect the farmers to make a contribution to the network; they will plan on a certain density of water-delivery structures per square mile and will then expect the farmers to dig ditches to take the waters from the delivery points to their own fields. Here frequently the bargaining constellation characteristic for highways and electric power is reversed, particularly when irrigation merely regularizes and supplements the existing water supply: the farmer will often sit tight and not undertake the investment outlays assigned him by the planners, and the irrigation authorities will eventually be forced to extend the network and to dig the missing ditches at their own expense. This sequence was observed both in the irrigation area of the Damodar Valley and quite prominently in Thailand's Chao Phya project which in 1962 required a special "ditches and dykes" loan from the World Bank to assure full utilization of the irrigation potential created by the larger structures previously completed.

It will be appreciated that the concept we are looking into here—substitutability of private for public sector outlays in the production of various categories of goods and services—is fairly basic to the operation of any economy.[20] We will be able to deal here only with a few aspects of the problem that are related to our interest in the behavior of investment projects under varying structural conditions.

The usual advantages of lack of latitude—that it facilitates decision making and goal setting and minimizes slippage and poor performance—certainly exist in this situation and are even reinforced by a further consideration: when there is sub-

20. I say "of any economy" rather than "of a mixed economy" because the same problem exists in a socialist economy. While the two cooperating sectors (say, highways and trucks) cannot here be identified with the public and private sectors, they are still decision-making centers largely independent of each other, and this independence is a sufficient condition for the problems discussed in the text to arise.

stantial latitude—substitutability of public for private outlays
—there may be considerable bargaining, explicit or implicit,
about fair shares to be contributed by each sector and, in the
process, valuable time—and mutual good will—may be lost,
as was indeed the case in both the Indian and Thai irrigation
projects.

In spite of these arguments against latitude, the presence of
a substantial degree of latitude cannot be unambiguously considered a drawback that will merely induce slippage and nothing else. For, just as in the preceding section a slippage on
quality permitted an increase in quantity, so here the public
sector's reneging on its conventional share will, by assumption,
elicit an increase in the private sector's share, with results for
resource allocation and growth that are not necessarily undesirable.

Again, some very simple analytics are helpful. In Figure 2
we are assuming that a certain desired volume of transportation or other services can be produced by different combinations of private and public outlays. These different combinations will result in an isoquant of conventional shape for road
transport, whereas the rectangular shape of the air transport
isoquant indicates the lack of substitutability of private for
public outlays. With both axes measured in dollars, the minimum cost combination lies at point P of tangency of the isoquant with a line forming an angle of 45 degrees with the two
axes. If prices paid by the public and private sectors correctly
reflect opportunity costs, then P represents the best possible
combination of public and private outlay in the production of
the desired volume of transportation services. The question is
now: how is such a point reached? In contrast to what happens
within a profit-maximizing firm which has an incentive to
equalize the marginal productivities of a dollar's worth of inputs, no simple mechanism is available for similarly equalizing

FIGURE 2. *Combinations of Public and Private Outlays for Various Services.*

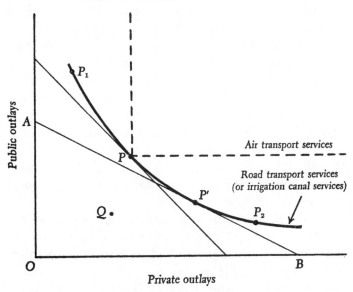

Private outlays

the marginal contributions of the public and private sectors. It is easy to see, in fact, that there are good reasons why simple technological conventions and rules-of-thumb dominate this field, for in their absence highly unstable situations could result. While the public and private sectors have, in a sense, a common interest in achieving a satisfactory volume of production (of, say, transportation services), each sector also has normally an interest in minimizing its own contribution and in maximizing thereby that of the other party. The attempt of each to minimize its contribution may then in fact result in a far lower production volume, such as is shown by point Q, than the mutually desired one. This is essentially the story of irrigation projects when public authorities try to "get away" with digging only the main laterals.

The conflict and bargaining situation here described clearly belongs in the class of half-antagonistic, half-cooperative games that have been thoroughly analyzed in Schelling's *Strategy of Conflict*. His conclusion was that in such bargaining or mixed-motive games, as he called them, the nature of the solution is powerfully influenced by the presence of "some obvious focus for agreement, some strong suggestion contained in the situation itself," or "a mutually identifiable resting place."[21]

In the implicit bargaining between the private and public sectors about their appropriate contributions to the production of goods and services, some "strong suggestion contained in the situation itself" is usually present as a result of the division of labor between the two sectors and of fixed and accepted standards of road and irrigation canal construction. In developed countries, however, such standards are not arbitrary, but are the result of prolonged interaction between the two sectors, for example, between the builders of highways and their users. Given interest group pressures and the often politically inspired desire to provide satisfactory service, on the one hand, and the institutional restraints on undue waste of public funds, on the other, the public sector will hopefully provide facilities that will neither be excessively generous nor obviously throw a disproportionate burden of the total cost on the private users. Under these conditions, a tendency to work toward the point P of minimal total cost may well assert itself in the long run even though the division of labor between the public and private sectors is embodied in rigid rules and standards that do not seem to be amenable to marginal adjustments.

When the standards prevailing in the developed countries for the division of labor between the public and private sectors are transferred to the less developed countries, it is quite likely that the solutions that have been worked out will prove inade-

21. Pp. 68, 71, 89.

quate. A tendency to depart from the accepted standards may represent an attempt to find a more appropriate solution, rather than mere slippage. Thus an underdeveloped country may have adopted initially a division of labor in two different activities, say road transport and irrigation, indicated by points P_1 or P_2 with too much and too little, respectively, being contributed by the public sector. An attempt to move away from these points in the direction of P is to be commended. In other words, the highway authorities' decision not to maintain a highway in quite the extravagant specifications to which it was built and the irrigation authorities' decision to meet the farmers halfway by digging additional ditches may both be moves toward a social optimum.

It could even be argued that the appropriate division of labor between the public and private sectors in underdeveloped countries will tend to diverge systematically from that in an advanced economy. It is a principal characteristic of underdeveloped countries that the tax base is very narrow, that tax morality is poor, and that collection costs are high so that the public sector is even more starved of funds than Galbraith has shown it to be in affluent societies. Hence, the rationing of funds is even stricter in the public than in the private sector and the marginal public fund dollar may well make a higher contribution to social production than the marginal dollar spent by the private sector. If this is so, the norms prevailing in the advanced countries should be altered and some substitution of private for public funds in the joint production of goods and services would be justified in underdeveloped countries. This consideration is reinforced when the opportunity cost of private investment spending can be assumed to be lower than its money cost: for example, spending on either education or trucks seems to have such a pre-eminent and almost unique place in the preferences of Africans for productive investment that the alternatives to it are home building at best, and otherwise luxury consumption (bigger wedding feasts) or leisure (less production of cash crops for the market).

In terms of Figure 2, the public dollar can be given a higher scarcity value than the private dollar by replacing the 45 degree line as the exchange ratio between the two sectors by a line such as *AB*. The resulting optimal point on the isoquant for roads naturally moves in a southeasterly direction to a point such as *P'*, indicating the desirability of a shift of expenditures from the public to the private sector, *combined with an increase in total spending.* This increase can be rational under the assumptions stated above, but it will of course lead to seemingly justified accusations of counter-productive skimping and penny-pinching against the public sector.

Whatever changes in the traditional norms for the division of total cost of transportation and other services between the private and public sectors may be needed, it is important that a new conventional "mutually identifiable resting place" for that division be defined rapidly. Any prolonged lack of such a place opens the door to the danger that each of the parties may hold back in the expectation that the other will "take up the slack"—with obviously most damaging results for economic progress.

As our inquiry into latitude is drawing to a close, we are a long way from the attractive simplicity with which the concept was presented in my *Strategy of Economic Development.* There I celebrated lack of latitude (primarily with respect to quality): it would force an underdeveloped country to do a job right and teach it performance, maintenance, and other virtues that could then be applied in the many other tasks where latitude was present. As a result of a more thorough exploration of the concept, we have now acquired a more qualified or perhaps an ambivalent position: while lack of latitude retains the great advantage of determinateness, of preventing mere slippage, of accelerating decision making, and in general of providing project directors and managers with firm discipline and guideposts for action, the presence of latitude has in some situations been shown to foster training in rational decision making or the adaptation of imported models of economic behavior to local conditions and requirements.

In any event, the concepts of latitude and discipline have turned out to be surprisingly useful as a key to the understanding of many aspects of project behavior. In fact, additional observations about the comparative advantages of latitude and lack of latitude will find their place in the next chapter.

CHAPTER FOUR

Project Design:
Trait-Taking and Trait-Making

THE ANALYSIS of project behavior has so far proceeded as fairly pure science, even though we have occasionally
come upon practical hints in the course of our observations on
uncertainty and latitude. We are now turning to a more direct
attack on what must clearly be an important part of the present
study, namely considerations on the choice, design, and appraisal of projects.

The general outcome of our discussion on uncertainty and
latitude for these matters is not free from ambiguity. For example, it might seem wise for a country lacking in technical
sophistication to shun projects surrounded by a great deal of
what has been termed technological supply uncertainty. Such
advice would evoke two objections.

First, it is by no means sure that it is feasible for the country
to substitute another equally good project for the uncertainty-
ridden one. In Uruguay, for example, the livestock project's
potential for permitting the economy to turn from stagnation
to expansion as a result of increased foreign exchange earnings
was wholly unrivalled. Because of the limited number of projects that are being readied for decision taking at any one time,
the considerations on project behavior so far discussed will
have their principal use not as selection or rejection criteria,
but rather as hopefully valuable indications to the project

128

planners and operators about the dangers and opportunities in store for projects on which decisions must be taken. This does not mean, of course, that occasionally the kind of considerations on which we are concentrating could not make the difference between selection and rejection of a project. One such case can be cited from among our sample. If the arguments which have already been gathered (pp. 46 and 109) on the comparative merits of railway and highway transportation in a country like Nigeria are added to those that still remain to be made (pp. 140–48), the decision to build the Maiduguri extension of the Nigerian Railway Corporation looks highly questionable in retrospect.[1]

Secondly and more fundamentally, in many cases there is considerable ambiguity about the *direction* our observations should impart to the investment decision. It could be argued that a country without much experience in solving technological problems should stay away from projects requiring a large capability in this regard. But the opposite course can also be defended: how will the country ever learn about technology if it does not tackle technologically complex and problem-rich tasks? In this reasoning a certain "unfitness" of the project for a country becomes an additional and strong argument for undertaking it; for the project, *if it is successful*, will be valuable not only because of its physical output but even more because of the social and human changes it will have wrought.

---

1. It must be kept in mind that at the time of the decision to build the railway, there was no clearcut highway alternative. The railroad had been surveyed; hence the extension, unlike some alternative highway projects, was ready to be undertaken. It is always difficult to argue that some nebulous alternative is better than what is being proposed in concrete detail, and this must have been especially so when the World Bank was anxious to become involved in the economic development of Africa's most populous country.

This sort of ambiguity affects even those of our observations that point to the likelihood of corruption in a certain type of project; it could well be argued that the only way to make any headway in fighting corruption is to have projects where there is latitude for corruption; for without such latitude, how can a measure of immunity from corruption ever be acquired?

The Dilemma of Design

The problem that is being discussed here raises in fact the basic dilemma of project design in an underdeveloped country. To formulate it quite generally, we posit an underdeveloped state or status quo with a number of negative attributes or "lacks" (lack of capital, of skills, of willingness to grant promotions or permits in accordance with merit, of ability to mediate conflicts between different social or ethnic groups, etc.) and a desired better state in which at least one, and perhaps several, of these attributes have become positive or less negative. The dilemma of project design is then the following: if the project is planned, built, and operated on the basis of certain negative attributes of the status quo, taking them for granted, as inevitable and unchangeable, it may miss important opportunities for effecting positive changes in these attributes—on the contrary, it may even confirm and strengthen them. The achievements of the project would then be far below what they might have been and the net result could even be negative from the point of view of some "social progress function." The project planners will stand convicted as men without imagination who do not really believe in change and perhaps do not desire it. If, on the other hand, success in the construction and operation of the project is made to hinge on a prior or concurrent or subsequent change in some of the attributes of backwardness, then the project's fate becomes a wager; if the wager is lost, so that the needed change does not occur and the project's success is thereby jeopardized, the project planners will be accused of ignoring local circumstances, traditions, and sociopolitical structure and of incorrigible naivete and lack of realism in general.

The art of project design consists of course in escaping from this dilemma. Implanting a project in an underdeveloped country implies (1) a decision to accept some status quo traits as temporarily unchangeable characteristics of the environment that will mold the project, and (2) a decision to consider others as subject to and ready for the kind of changes that are required for making a success of the project.

With the help of some apt terminology from price theory, the project may therefore be said to act at the same time as "trait-taker" and as "trait-maker": the decision which traits to "take," that is, to accept (because they are considered unchangeable) and which ones to make (by changing existing or creating new traits) is crucial to project design and success. Yet it is hardly ever spelled out. Should it be? Would it perhaps be useful for the project planners to ask themselves whether changes in project design might not make it possible for them to act a bit more as trait-makers and a bit less as trait-takers or vice versa? Could not an explicit analysis of this usually implicit decision reveal to them on one occasion that they would be rash in assuming the role of trait-makers while on another they would be throwing away a precious opportunity by not doing so? To facilitate this sort of analysis, some scrutiny of these concepts is necessary.

TRAIT-TAKING. Under trait-taking we are actually lumping together a number of quite different activities. First there is of course the possibility that the locally available traits are perfectly suitable for the construction and operation of the project. This seems a happy situation, but it will be noted that a project that would be trait-taking in all its dimensions would leave the environment entirely untouched, except for the additional output. It would therefore largely fail as an agent for change.

The opposite kind of trait-taking is more interesting: here the available traits are so far from satisfying the needs of project construction and operation that any short-term possibility of generating needed skills and inputs locally is dismissed; hence they are *imported* from abroad or from the more advanced regions of the same country.[2] This is the kind of trait-taking that may become trait-reinforcing: the local people whose inability to perform certain tasks is taken for granted and as unchangeable may come to be systematically excluded (especially if their skin is of a different color from that of the immigrants or "expatriates") from the skilled positions and occupations by the newcomers who will acquire an interest in being retained as "indispensable" in the elite positions they have come to occupy. Similarly, imports of needed material inputs may discourage or destroy any incipient local production. These are familiar mechanisms, well described by the concepts "cumulative sequence" and "self-fulfilling prophecy."

That any import, however "additional" and "temporary," can develop this tendency to further worsen the local supply situation has been illustrated in recent years by the adverse effects, reported from several countries, of United States surplus food shipments on local food growing. It has also been plausibly argued that the importation of capital, originally justified by the low level of local capital formation, can stunt the growth of a domestic capital market and may be relied on,

2. The difficulties of African economic development have been analyzed in terms of these two opposite and equally unsatisfactory types of trait-taking by R. E. Baldwin in "Export Technology and Development from a Subsistence Level," *Economic Journal*, Vol. 73 (March 1963), pp. 73–80.

because of both vested interests and institutional inertia, for much longer than is necessary.[3]

Imports do not, however, have only these stunting effects. Such effects are the first to assert themselves and they may well continue to dominate the scene in the absence of deliberate intervention of opposing policies. But today this intervention is virtually certain to take place, as is witnessed by the various and widespread import substitution and "-ization" (Nigerianization, Indianization, etc.) policies. In many cases, the fastest or even only possible way of generating some local production, skill, or even attitude is to import it as an object lesson for local imitators and learners.[4] Trait-taking can thus be made to entrain trait-making. It would therefore be quite wrong, besides being hopelessly impractical, to oppose on principle the kind of trait-taking that reacts to the absence or shortage of a desired trait by importing it. But it seems to be a fact that such imports never leave the local scene quite alone: they either stunt or stimulate it, and often do both, in succession.

The fact that trait-taking-cum-importing often entrains trait-making at a later stage makes for a different valuation of importing for purposes of project construction than for operation. Trait-taking through importing (of material inputs or human skills) for the purposes of operating a project is relatively harmless since in due course the imports can be replaced by domestic inputs so that trait-taking will give way to trait-making. The situation is rather different for construction, especially when the project is one of a kind—say, the harnessing of the country's only large river by a dam. Trait-taking-cum-importing is unlikely to lead here to much trait-making.

3. J. Knapp, "Capital Exports and Growth," *Economic Journal*, Vol. 67 (September 1957), pp. 432–44.
4. See *Strategy of Economic Development*, Chap. 7.

There simply is not enough time for import-substitution activities to follow in the wake of the imports, and the valuable experience in organizing a large-scale construction effort and many other benefits from trait-making during construction are lost to the country in which such a unique project is built. Only when there is a long and continuous sequence of similar projects will import substitution have its chance once again, as was shown particularly well in the construction of the successive thermoelectric power plants of the Damodar Valley Corporation: whereas the first plant at Bokaro was built entirely by foreign contractors and under the supervision of foreign engineers, only one lonely foreign consulting engineer was to be seen around the huge new plant at Chandrapura.

The two varieties of trait-taking so far discussed—the trait is perfectly suited to the task, hence used, and the trait is wholly unsuited, hence left alone and replaced by imports of one kind or another—are both associated with a high degree of certainty: the "right" traits either are available locally or are brought in from outside. The various uncertainties of Chapter 2 enter the picture with the third variety of trait-taking: it occurs when substitution of the local traits through imports is not possible or is deemed unnecessary or uneconomical while, on the other hand, the local traits are not the same as the ones that are normally used or are known from previous project experience.

Any adaptation of production processes (or of products) to locally available raw materials and skills or to locally existing factor proportions would fall into this category. The use of "rugged" machinery because workers' skills are low or of labor-intensive methods because labor is cheap are examples of this adaptation. While trait-taking in these cases hardly would result in any deterioration of local resources and abilities, it can be and has been argued that it is growth-stunting; this would be particularly so if unequivocally "backward" traits were taken to be unchangeable and if production processes and factor payments were adjusted to accommodate them.[5] On the other hand, it is occasionally found that such nonconventional resources as are locally available can satisfactorily and perhaps even advantageously be substituted for conventional inputs. This outcome would suddenly make trait-taking very appealing: it would permit a country to put the stamp of its own resource endowment and personality on its undertakings, and might even make it hit in the process on its comparative advantage when it had considered its own resources as strictly second-rate and perhaps as backward.

Another possible outcome of the attempt at trait-taking under uncertainty is of course that it would not work: The suitability and versatility of the local traits has been overestimated and it is found that they need to be either replaced by imports after all or modified. In this case, trait-making takes over once again.

TRAIT-MAKING. One of the dangers in trait-taking is that the undesirable or backward traits that are taken for granted in planning a project actually become more strongly entrenched and that the project thus fails to generate as much progressive change as is within its grasp. The risk in trait-making is that the desirable traits which are required for an adequate functioning of the project will simply not be "made"—that is, learned in time—with dire results for the project's success. If that risk is too big, it is best to revert to some form of trait-taking (for example, importing) or to give up the project altogether.

Under what conditions is the risk sufficiently small that trait-making becomes a practical possibility? The most obvious

5. Hla Myint, *The Economics of the Developing Countries* (London: Hutchinson, 1964), Chap. 4.

answer is that many traits, from simple skills to administrative ability, can be slowly learned "on the job" or alongside it. The fact that these traits are not yet available in the desired quantity and quality at the inception of the project can mean simply that the cost of construction and operation of the project should make allowance for the inevitable learning process to which outside education and training will of course be expected to make an important contribution. It is precisely because much trait-making proceeds through gradual "on the job" learning that latitude for poor performance can be a welcome attribute of projects. The idea is that one starts at the poor end of the scale and slowly improves his performance. This expectation has long been a principal argument for infant-industry protection. The gradual learning that is possible when latitude is present is perhaps to be preferred to the somewhat hectic and forced change in behavior compelled by lack of latitude since the changes wrought in the former way are likely to be more lasting and also more transferable to areas other than the one in and for which the behavior was actually learned.[6]

Unfortunately trait-making is not always that easy. In the first place, some needed traits are frequently so far removed

6. I must relate here a personal observation: While living in Bogotá in the fifties, I observed with some surprise that the Bogotanos would show the utmost discipline in queuing up for city buses—even as few as two people would often stand in a rigid line. Upon inquiring about the reason for this "modern" behavior, I was told that the habit had been literally beaten into the citizenry by the army which after the famous 1948 riots, when almost all the streetcars were burned, provided urban transportation in army trucks. Significantly, the discipline that was thus learned under duress had no visible spillover effects on behavior in general, not even under favorable circumstances: even though it is well known that the number of tickets sold for an airplane flight cannot exceed the number of seats available, the opening of the gate at the Bogotá airport frequently gave rise to real stampedes.

from the country's current technical attainments, sociopolitical conditions, and cultural values that their gradual acquisition, even if it were possible, would cost far more than trait-
taking-cum-importing.

Secondly, one can at times not be wholly certain that the
alien attitudes, types of behavior, and skills will ever be learned.
For their acquisition does not proceed so much through gradual on or off the job learning as through *changes in values*
which are often abrupt as well as subject to sharp oscillations.
Take for example the matter of making job appointments in
accordance with merit and objective qualification, rather than
on the basis of political, family, tribal, or religious affinity.
This change in criteria is not likely to come about through
gradual learning in the manner in which a language or a skill
can be slowly acquired. Even though, in practice, the number
of appointments made in accordance with "objective" or
achievement standards may increase gradually, the turnaround
in values is bound to be abrupt so that at one point yesterday's
exceptions are felt as today's rules, and vice versa. It is also
likely that before the new behavior norms are completely
internalized and consistently adhered to, there will be frequent reversions to the old behavior, because of the tensions
between the old and the new ethos; such vacillating behavior,
characteristic of a transitional stage, is again vastly different
from that of a person who is halfway through a course for lathe
operators.

According to Talcott Parsons, an actor must commit himself wholly to one side of the basic Parsonian dichotomies
or pattern variables (universalism-particularism, ascription-
achievement, etc.) before he can even act.[7] Whether or not

7. Talcott Parsons and Edward A. Shils (eds.), *Toward a General Theory of Action: Theoretical Foundations for the Social Sciences* (Har-per & Row [Harper Torchbook edition], 1962), pp. 76–77.

this postulate is accepted, it is certain that the acquisition of some traits is more a matter of one-time choice, commitment, and turnaround than of gradual learning.

It would seem then that trait-making must withdraw from the areas where its success is highly uncertain. No doubt, in many cases where the wrong traits prevail (wrong from the point of view of the project's success) trait-taking is the only rational course, pending general sociopolitical and value changes in the society in which the project is to be built and operated. It is within this scheme that our earlier partiality for lack of latitude (or discipline) is vindicated: some precious terrain may be wrested from trait-taking and be taken over by trait-making in projects whose structure so compellingly requires the desired traits that in their absence high penalties would be incurred or the task simply could not be undertaken at all. Lack of latitude as a structural characteristic of the task is particularly conducive to the adoption of those traits that are taken up as a result of a full-fledged, one-time commitment rather than of gradual learning. The radical demands of a task with no latitude for poor performance not only facilitate such turnarounds in values and behavior, but provide a strong barrier against any backsliding.

If it is introduced at the right time, an exacting, disciplinarian technology can produce an effect very similar to that in the Southern United States of federal legislation or, better, court orders on desegregation: these orders act as alibis and face-saving devices for those in the South who are about ready to shed traditional segregationist behavior or practices but could not do so on their own because of the prevailing community ethos to which they have long paid homage or lip-service. One of the greatest values of projects introducing a technology with little or no latitude for poor performance into an underdeveloped country is similarly that they are uniquely suited to permit open commitments to modern values among the builders and operators of the project.

We must end this brief dissection of our new concepts on a cautionary note. Trait-making cannot pretend to displace trait-taking in any and all projects where lack of latitude prevails. As this lack often means simply that a high penalty will have to be paid if the needed traits are not acquired, a judgment will have to be made in each case whether the chances of successful trait-making are good enough to make the penalties of failure an acceptable risk. But then, our point was not to supersede trait-taking entirely; it is rather that project planners can materially enlarge the area of trait-making and can in fact undertake certain projects they would otherwise be well advised to postpone or not take up at all by enlisting the help of tasks characterized by lack of latitude in the kind of trait-making that proceeds discontinuously rather than gradually.

It turns out that latitude and lack of latitude can both be valuable in facilitating that learning or acquisition of needed skills and traits which we have called here trait-making. But each has been shown to have specialized functions: latitude is attuned to gradual learning, whereas lack of latitude has a special affinity for the changes that take place through discontinuous commitments to new values and types of behavior.

Implicit Trait-Making: A Failure in Nigeria

Looking at projects with the help of the concepts of trait-taking and trait-making may improve their design in the following ways: (a) it may reveal some areas where trait-making can advantageously and without undue risk replace trait-taking; and (b) it may reveal other areas where the project is (explicitly or implicitly) trait-making to an extent that is either wholly unrealistic or that, if it is to be successful, requires far more attention than the project planners are giving it.

It would be practically impossible to document conclusively, from our project histories, the first category of improvements in project design. To affirm, upon looking back, that a project has not produced as much progressive change as was within its grasp would require one to make a most difficult judgment on benefits that might have accrued if certain changes in project design and organization had been made.

On the other hand, we have some rather striking examples of the second category in a wide range of experiences where trait-making has met with either failure or success. These were not cases where trait-making was consciously attempted and did or did not succeed, but situations in which the project planners were unaware to what extent the good fortune of their project was implicitly premised on trait-making, that is, on making over the social, economic, and human reality of their country in one way or another. These cases of implicit trait-making illustrate one of the preferred modes of operation of the Hiding Hand—and also one of the more dangerous. For this reason, project planners ought to become sensitive to situations in which the amount of trait-making required for the success of a project is substantial, particularly when the contemplated project must compete against another activity that is not nearly as demanding.

The most elaborate case in point is that of the Nigerian Railway Corporation. Four of Nigeria's outstanding characteristics (traits) over the past several years have been (1) tribal or "group" tension and antagonism; (2) the vigorous use of economic power to attain political influence and, in turn, of political power to improve the economic position of the power-holder, his family, and his clan or tribe; (3) widespread corruption; and (4) rapid Nigerianization, that is, replacement of expatriate by local personnel.

We shall now show that each of the traits made the "lorries" increasingly able to compete successfully against the railways. Thus a decision to invest nevertheless substantial amounts in railway expansion could have been justified only if there was some reasoned confidence that some of these traits could be changed or that the advantages they conferred upon the lorries could somehow be neutralized.

As briefly noted in Chapter 2, the tribal and regional animosities characteristic of Nigeria have a striking, though often unrealized, differential impact on the efficiency of the railways in comparison to that of highway transport. The integrated railway network of Nigeria operates in all the regions of the country and is run from a central headquarters in the outskirts of Lagos. Being a nationwide organization, it is necessarily shot through with all the tensions and antagonisms the nation itself is experiencing. Before independence most of the key jobs of the railway were held by expatriate British personnel, but with independence and stepped-up Nigerianization the problem of tribal balance within the organization was bound to arise. In principle, two opposite types of solution to the problem are conceivable. On the one hand, a very determined attempt can be made to attain tribal balance throughout the organization; in that case, efficiency will be seriously affected (a) because in the interests of balance, unqualified personnel from the more backward areas will be given jobs and promotions; (b) because once balance is more or less achieved, promotions must be handled strictly on a seniority rather than on a merit basis so as to minimize accusations of favoritism; (c) because there are bound to be frictions and simple problems of communication between people unused to cooperating.

The other possibility is that considerations of tribal balance are disregarded either in the interests of efficiency or because of the top managers' partiality for members of their own group (both factors operated in Nigeria). In that case, however, the railway's fortunes will also be gravely jeopardized: the fact that it is the fief of one group or tribe will make the railway highly unpopular with the remaining groups in the country and, since officials of the regional governments have considerable control over the movement of bulk merchandise (as a result of marketing board schemes which are set up on a regional rather than national base), the railway will lose customers because of hostility and discrimination.

None of these difficulties affect the competing mode, transport by trucks. Trucking is carried on by a very large number of small to medium-sized firms owning from one to perhaps twenty vehicles, and each firm is free to hire whomsoever it pleases. Trucking firms are either Ibo, Yoruba, Hausa, or Lebanese, but each firm is a homogenous unit unburdened by problems of tribal rivalries and hostility. This is a prime reason for the vigorous development of trucking in West Africa and its ability to compete successfully against the railways. Trucking is here trait-taking (the tribal divisions are accommodated and easily lived with) while railroading must be trait-making to be successful, that is, its success is predicated on the possibility of overcoming tribal antagonisms at least within the railway organization.

The second Nigerian trait relevant to an appraisal of rail versus road competition is the vigorous use of economic power for attaining political influence and, in turn, of political power for economic improvement of the powerholder, his (extended) family, and his tribal group. This trait also works in favor of the trucking industry. The reason is simple: owning a truck is one of the few roads to economic success in Nigeria. By stimulating truck transportation, highways make an essential contribution to entrepreneurship and social mobility.[8] But they

8. George W. Wilson et al., *The Impact of Highway Investment on Development* (Brookings Institution, 1966), Chap. 7.

do more: by causing an economically prominent group to arise, they create ipso facto an important political power base for the trucking industry. A large number of ministers and members of parliament or members of their families will have a substantial stake in the industry and will therefore be actively on the lookout for its interests. Any attempt at restraining it by "coordinating" rail and road transport is therefore likely to be blocked. Instead, given again the considerable role of regional agencies such as marketing boards, the trucking interests are able to obtain preferential treatment in the allocation of cargo. The railways, even though—or rather because—they are a public corporation and are therefore nobody's direct and personal concern, are wholly unable to match the strong appeal the trucking industry has for the politician; only when they are running up a disastrous deficit, as in 1965, will the government take notice and adopt some remedial measures. Once again the trucking industry thrives with the "trait" we are discussing, whereas successful operation of the railways would require a change in the trait, that is, in the way in which economic policy is in fact made in Nigeria—and it is easy to understand that such a change would require nothing less than a substantial overhaul of the country's economic and social structure.

A third trait that affects far more adversely the fortunes of the railways than those of the competing mode is corruption. One reason (already given) is that corruption in the building or rebuilding of the railway or in the acquisition of modern rolling stock will debilitate the discipline, efficiency, and morale of the organization for operational purposes, whereas the building and repair of highways is handled by an organization wholly distinct from the users, so that any malpractices in construction and maintenance are of no concern to the truck operators that ride on them. Moreover, the trucks, being often driven by the owner or the owner's brother, are far better at taking on-the-spot decisions to distribute small favors to port authority and other officials who influence the allocation of incoming freight between the railways and the trucks; as noted before, the railways, or rather some of their employees, are able to join the fun by exacting additional payments from hard-pressed customers anxious to move their goods, but they are clumsy, like any large-scale bureaucratic organization, when it comes to handing out funds and to authorizing any expense that is not duly receipted. Hence trucks not only suffer less in their efficiency from the state of corruption than the railroads, but also know how to play the corruption game better. Once again, they are well adapted to "taking" the trait, whereas successful operation of the railroads would require the "unmaking" of the prevailing trait and the "making" of the opposite one.

A fourth factor working against the railways in the Nigerian situation was Nigerianization. The replacement of expatriate by local personnel is likely to have some adverse impact on efficiency at least during a transitional phase, and since the railways relied on large numbers of expatriates, Nigerianization was bound to create managerial and technical problems for them. The trucks were in the hands of either Nigerians or Lebanese, and while the latter were exposed to increasing competition from the Nigerians, there was no official program of nationalization. For Nigerianization not to affect the competitive position of the railways, it would have had to be conducted with a wisdom and moderation that can hardly be expected in human affairs.

Finally we may consider a further, more narrowly economic effect—an expansion of the rail or road system—on the comparative efficiency of operations of the two modes. An expansion of the railways, such as the three-hundred-mile Maiduguri extension, makes additional claims on the decision-making ability of the central administration and other "overhead" factors which are likely to be in fixed and rather scarce supply. As a result, such an addition is likely to lead to some deterioration of the services the railways used to offer on the old network—there simply will be more of a probability that rolling stock and key personnel will be at the wrong place at the wrong time and that important decisions will suffer more delay. When, on the other hand, more road mileage is built, there will be no decreasing-returns effect since, maintenance apart, the roads essentially run themselves without any central direction. Here again, railroad building can be said to betray an ambition to be a trait-maker—to operate successfully the enlarged network requires a concomitant increase in the ability and skills of management, whereas road building assumes no such development, except in the maintenance organization.

It is perhaps puzzling that all of these factors should conspire in a single direction, to harm the competitive position of the railways vis-à-vis the trucks. But it is even stranger that these important consequences of economic, social, and political structure have hardly ever been adverted to by the many experts who have studied competition in the transport industry in Nigeria.[9] The persistent failure to notice these numerous and very real links between sociopolitical structure and project behavior suggests serious and systematic neglect of an area that can be crucial to the performance of the project. Bringing, as they do, new activities into a pre-existing environment, development projects are likely to imply far more would-be trait-making than is commonly realized, and a principal task of the project analyst is to uncover the most significant economic

9. See, for example, the report of the Stanford Research Institute, *The Economic Coordination of Transport in Nigeria*, February 1961 (processed). Honorable mention must be made of the study by E. K. Hawkins, *Road Transport in Nigeria: A Study of African Enterprise* (Oxford University Press, 1958), which shows an excellent appreciation of the expansive power of the trucking industry at a time when the idea that trucks could seriously compete with railroads in long-distance hauling was still widely dismissed.

and sociopolitical changes on which the success of the project is implicitly premised. Once it is understood what these required changes are, the question is of course whether it is realistic to expect them to occur in advance or in the wake of the project; in Nigeria if there had been better appreciation of the conditions that make the performance of railways poorer than that of roads, it would have been realized that most of these conditions are deeply embedded in the present phase of Nigerian development.

At this point, however, the question may well arise whether highways and "lorries" are perhaps accommodating too easily all of Nigeria's current traits, desirable and undesirable, and whether a complete "surrender" to the highways would not amount precisely to a victory for tribalism, corruption, etc., when with the railways there would remain at least a fighting chance that some of the more undesirable and progress-stunting traits will come under attack.

The reply to this question comes in several parts. In describing the special difficulties the railways experience in coping with present-day Nigerian conditions, we were noting an objective situation which will lower the level of performance of the railways in comparison to that of the highways; it was our contention that transport investment decisions should take this situation into account. If it is believed that the railways can usefully make a contribution to nation-building, serve as a school for cooperation among the tribes in a large organization, etc., then the benefits to be expected from such learning may conceivably justify a subsidy to the railways.

The case for such a subsidy becomes rather problematical, however, precisely because of the presence of a competing mode. In the first place, highways are themselves quite good at spawning considerable external benefits such as social mobility, entrepreneurship, and wider horizons in general. Secondly, the presence of a ready alternative to rail transport makes it less, rather than more, likely that the weaknesses of the railways will be fought rather than indulged. With truck and bus transportation available, a deterioration in rail service is not nearly so serious a matter as if the railways held a monopoly for long-distance transport—it can be lived with for a long time without arousing strong public pressures for the basic and politically difficult or even explosive reforms in administration and management that would be required. This may be the reason public enterprise, not only in Nigeria but in many other countries, has strangely been at its weakest in sectors such as transportation and education where it is subjected to competition: instead of stimulating improved or top performance, the presence of a ready and satisfactory substitute for the services public enterprise offers merely deprives it of a precious feedback mechanism that operates at its best when the customers are securely locked in. For the management of public enterprise, always fairly confident that it will not be let down by the national treasury, may be less sensitive to the loss of revenue due to the switch of customers to a competing mode than to the protests of an aroused public that has a vital stake in the service, has no alternative, and will therefore "raise hell."

Put differently: Intolerably bad service becomes tolerable when there is an alternative mode supplying approximately the same service; and since "there is nothing worse than a moderate evil," as Keynes has said,[10] the chances for action being taken against intolerably bad service or for the service not becoming intolerably bad in the first place are better when it is supplied in conditions of monopoly.

In terms of our earlier categories, the presence of a competing mode then appears to provide the railways not so much

10. And he continued: "If wasps and rats were hornets and tigers we should have exterminated them before now." A Treatise on Money (Macmillan, 1930), Vol. 2, p. 175.

with a spur for good performance as with a special kind of latitude for poor performance. From all that has been said about the kind of handicaps affecting the railways, it is clear that we have here a prime example of the project in which improved performance depends on a once-and-for-all commitment to new values and attitudes rather than gradual learning of some new skills; and, as was explained earlier in this chapter, the chances that this commitment will be made and observed are the better the smaller the latitude for poor performance. Hence, once it is understood that competition functions here as latitude rather than as spur, the chances for the railways to become a school for noncorruption, for coexistence among the various tribes, and for similar fundamental shifts in behavior must be considered rather poor, at least in the absence of specially designed institutional devices.

For the same reasons, conditions for achieving a satisfactory level of performance through successful trait-making are more favorable in public projects that supply a wholly new and unique type of service. This is fortunate, for frequently we do have to make a choice, not, as in the rail versus road alternative of Nigeria, between a severely trait-making project and one that is able to "swim" with all the existing traits while providing essentially the same output, but between investing in a project premised on extensive trait-making or doing nothing at all in the particular sector. To a considerable extent this is true of such projects as air transport, electric power generation, and telecommunications.

Entrained Trait-Making

Project analysts' neglect of the implicit trait-making aspects, ambitions, or premises of projects or, in other words, their insufficient appreciation of basic traits that must be either accommodated or eradicated but cannot be simply ignored is at the bottom of several of the more serious difficulties our projects have experienced. Besides the Nigerian case, we have referred to the situation in the Volturno Valley near Naples where success of the irrigation was found to be conditioned on breaking the stranglehold the "Camorra" has over the fruit and vegetable business in the region. Or we may refer to the early troubles of the Karnaphuli Paper Mill: the 1955 riot which cost several lives including that of the general manager of the mill, and the serious setback suffered by the mill as a result, must be attributed to the failure of the project planners to make full allowance for the ethnic sensitivities of the Bengali population of East Pakistan.

In relating, in the chapter on latitude, how projects in Peru and Uganda that remained underutilized too long almost "lost their souls"—that is, functioned, at least for some time, in a manner almost opposite to their planned purpose—we presented two cases of projects that set out to be trait-makers, but given the unanticipated resilience of the trait that was to be superseded, became in effect trait-takers, much against the intentions of the project planners. Such misadventures are again due to insufficient acquaintance with the existing structure whose toughness requires either surrender to it or skillful strategy aimed at fighting or subverting it.

Identification of the traits that must either be accommodated or be fought or subverted if a project is to be successful is of course no easy task; fortunately the lack of perceptiveness of the project planners in this regard is not always fraught with disastrous consequences, thanks to something akin to the Hiding Hand principle: while project planners tend to ignore or underestimate the extent of trait-making a project requires, and might well have refrained from undertaking it had they been better informed, it often turns out that the required trait can be generated and induced by the project itself or alongside the project. In the Uruguayan project, for example, improvement of the grasslands through implantation of more legumes was attacked essentially as a technical task, as was indeed natural in view of the important and difficult technical problems that had to be solved (see Chapter 2). Then, as various solutions gradually appeared as a result of research and experience, it became clear that full exploitation of the newly revealed opportunities required a great deal of day-to-day management, on-the-spot supervision, and delicate (that is, risky) decision making; in other words, technical change could come about only if it were accompanied by cultural or social transformation: the absentee landowner had to turn presentee unless he was either willing to hire a highly qualified and independent manager or could be made to rent or sell his land to others more willing to act as "modern" farmers. Actually, a number of participating landowners decided to live or to spend much more time on their properties in order to supervise personally the progress of the scheme. The newly worked out techniques permitted considerable individual variation and implied not only the use of modern machinery, but also continued scientific experimentation and the exercise of judgment. Thus, they contained an element of intellectual excitement and personal involvement that, added to the need to take good care of the additional investment, provided some compensation for foregoing life in the capital city.

Many landowners tried out the techniques because they were presented as both financially attractive and socially prestigeful; but once they had made the investment, they found they were obliged or desirous to change their way of life to a much larger extent than they had bargained for or anticipated. At the same time, the fact that another group of landowners refused to take advantage of the newly opened up opportunities (and thus were branded "lazy" and "routine-ridden") made the influential, progressive-landowner-dominated Honorary Commission willing to advocate fiscal measures that would penalize underutilization of the country's grazing lands. Here, then, is a situation where the attitudinal and social changes that are required for the technical discoveries to be fully utilized may not have to be put into place prior to, concurrently with, or in general separately from these discoveries. Rather, they are entrained by these discoveries which are taken up at first without the proper attitudes, almost as though "for play."

There are many similar situations where actors commit themselves to a technical innovation without realizing the extent to which this commitment *entrains* slowly and subtly, but irresistibly, additional changes in behavior; thus, it is not necessarily fatal not to have planned for these changes, even though they be essential for the success of the innovation. The extent to which the initial commitment can be relied on to produce the behavioral or social changes required to make the project yield its intended benefits varies once again sharply from one project and one technology to another. Even within a given project such entrainment effects can be remarkable in one direction and negligible in another. Thus, the installation of telephones in Ethiopia is said to have been outstandingly successful in replacing cash by credit transactions: before the telephone, contracts between exporters in the capital and merchants from the interior were concluded through face-to-face meetings accompanied by delivery of the merchandise, say coffee, and immediate hand-to-hand cash settlements; with the advent of the telephone, and the consequent replacement of physical by electrical voice-to-voice relationship, it became possible and necessary to enter into a commitment to buy coffee at a certain price long before the coffee was actually delivered; while in the West credit relationships were well established by the time the telephone was invented, in Ethiopia the spread of the credit system received a considerable impetus from the long-distance telephone whose use strongly insinuated a minimum of mutual trust among the subscribers if it were to be of any value to them.

On the other hand, an optimist might have expected the telephone to bring additional important changes: could it not lead, for example, to better and easier communication among various government departments and ministries and, hence, to less feuding and bureaucratic delay since officials would "pick up the phone" to settle an issue directly instead of communicating only via their superiors, their superiors' superiors, and so on until the matter must be decided by the Emperor? Fortunately, the financial success of the Ethiopian telecommunications project did not depend on induced changes of this sort, for according to the evidence I have come across, they have been minimal.

With our last remarks we have been using the concept of trait-making in a new context: we have applied it to the output of a project (the telephone call) rather than, as up to now, to the inputs and processes through which outputs are eventually produced or to the institutions, attitudes, and values required for efficient production. The concept of trait-taking could of course be similarly applied to the project's output. The telephone can, for example, be said to have an important trait-taking property in Ethiopia inasmuch as it accommodates an existing trait, namely the high degree of illiteracy: in this respect the telephone, a highly "modern" form of communication, is *less* of a trait-maker than the postal service, which is probably a major reason for its superior attraction and success. Returning for a moment to highway versus railway, the same relationship applies: the more modern mode—automotive vehicles, that is, with their flexible schedules, their bargaining, and the possibility to select a bus or truck with a friendly driver from one's own village or town—fits nicely in the existing pattern of life in Nigeria or, for that matter, many other developing countries; in all these respects, the nineteenth-century railways are more sternly trait-making. What we have here is in effect a curious association between the "degree of advancedness" of a technology and that technology's ability to fit right into nonmodern societies with a minimum of trait-making. It is most unlikely that this association holds over a wide range of technology, but insofar as it is valid for a few important transportation and communications media, it helps to account for the ease and alacrity with which developing countries are apt to leapfrog in these sectors.[11]

The Autonomous Agency as a Hybrid

Faced with the need or desire to implant "modern" activities into countries many of whose traits ought to be changed if these activities are to be conducted with any success, project planners have hit on a solution that partakes of both trait-taking and trait-making. They are willing to be trait-takers inasmuch as they give up as unrealistic any expectation that the traits that are incompatible with successful operation of the project could be eradicated in time in the society at large. On

11. In communications, this association has provided Marshall Mc-Luhan with one of his grander generalizations: With the invention of printing and other mechanical devices, Western culture has become visual, linear, and mechanical whereas "backward countries . . . still have much of their traditional oral culture that has the total unified 'field' character of our new electromagnetism." Hence, the latter "are much better able to confront and to understand electric technology." *Understanding Media: The Extensions of Man* (McGraw-Hill [McGraw-Hill Paperbacks edition], 1965), p. 27. To a considerable extent, McLuhan's book is an exploration—by his special intuitive technique—of the trait-making properties of individual "media."

the other hand, they are unwilling to forego or delay their project, so they attempt to set it up with all the required "modern" traits as an enclave protected by suitable safeguards against contamination by a hostile environment. The well-known technological dualism, so characteristic of the less developed countries, is thus being matched by dualism in the administrative, organizational, and value realms.

The administrative device embodying this intermediate solution is the *autonomous authority* or *agency*, which is designed to insulate the project from the country in general and from the rest of the public sector in particular. In the latter, inefficiency, inadequate salaries, frequent changes in key personnel and policies, nepotism, corruption, and "politics" are presumed to hold undisputed sway, whereas within the autonomous authority all of these practices are supposed to be banished and replaced by their virtuous opposites.

The idea that this could be accomplished through the magic wand of a simple administrative device has exerted such an appeal that recourse to the autonomous agency has become almost a standard reflex to a new or difficult task. The real limitations and hazards faced by such an agency go largely unnoticed. Yet they should be obvious on a priori grounds: after all, the device is almost a sleight-of-hand, an attempt at infiltrating something alien and new into an old structure with the help and connivance of that very structure—a tall order which can probably be carried out under some exceptionally favorable conditions (or as a result of careful "reformmongering") but hardly with the frequency and routine regularity with which such agencies are established around the world.[12]

12. This critique of the autonomous agency device as an easy remedy proceeds from much the same spirit as the one that is often made of proposals for land reform under conditions in which power is largely in the hands of the land owning interests. See *Journeys Toward Progress*, pp. 252 ff.

The task is then to understand the circumstances under which this administrative formula for making trait-taking and trait-making coexist will work and to become aware at the same time of some of the difficulties and pitfalls in store for it. Our projects, almost all of which have had recourse to the formula in one way or another, have several lessons to teach in this regard.

The establishment of the autonomous agency meets with far fewer difficulties than its successful operation. Yet establishment is by no means easy since the central administration is naturally reluctant to relinquish power or to accept establishment of a new activity somewhat removed from its direct control. It was argued in Chapter 2 under the heading of administrative difficulties that the reluctance to relinquish power is most easily overcome when the task to be undertaken contains a strong element of innovation. Most commonly and most obviously, innovation is of the technological kind, as in projects concerned with electric power, telecommunications, air transport, or the like. Here it is perhaps clearest to the policy makers that the requirements of technical skill and competence, of continuity, and of teamwork among people from diverse backgrounds are essential to success, and that the undertakings should therefore be kept from too close contact with wholly different environments.

The argument of technological complexity is occasionally reinforced by that of geographical "innovation" and isolation. We have already noted that typical site-bound projects—large river dams or new ports—have often provided a good basis for successful autonomous authorities, such as El Salvador's Lempa River Commission.

Social and administrative innovation often brings with it the establishment of new agencies or authorities: new ventures in regional development or in agrarian reform are today almost invariably organized in this form precisely because these are attempts at introducing into the existing social and administrative structure new elements that, it is felt, cannot be entrusted to "old-line" agencies. In the United States, the same process has of course become quite familiar since the New Deal.

So much for the areas in which there is a strong case for establishing autonomous agencies and in which they ought to have the best chances of success in operation. What, then, can go wrong? In the first place, the time may simply not be ripe for even so limited an advance as is implied by the creation of a modern "enclave." A number of autonomous agencies that were set up to infiltrate the old order by a new spirit have in fact been infiltrated in turn. One of the principal reasons autonomy is advocated is to acquire "insulation from politics" —that is, avoidance of politically motivated appointments, of nepotism, and of other practices detrimental to sound management. In a number of cases, however, the "autonomous agency" has shown a worse performance in this respect than the national government and its direct subdivisions. Government agencies often attempt, for the sake of political survival, to preserve a minimum of political, regional, or tribal balance; but an agency that is "off in a corner" may become the undisputed fief of one political party, tribe, or clan. This is exactly what happened in Nigeria with the railways which had been reorganized as an autonomous corporation in 1955 and which fell under the complete domination of one clan after independence. Another striking example is Brazil's São Francisco Valley Authority whose unglorious career I have described elsewhere.[13]

The symmetrically opposite danger threatening the success of the autonomous agency is that "insulation from politics" be taken too seriously as an overriding objective: the price of this

13. *Ibid.*, pp. 50–56.

insulation can be loss of easy access to political power, and this loss may be crippling, specially for agencies engaging in highly controversial social and administrative, rather than purely technological, innovation. The Damodar Valley Corporation found this out when it was locked in battle with the state of West Bengal over its irrigation and power programs and was unable to obtain the backing of the central government.

Another source of difficulty may also be mentioned. When, as was frequently the case in our sample, the autonomous agency has been established with some backing from international agencies and is a chosen instrument for channeling technical or financial assistance toward a country, it is frequently suspected within that country that the vaunted autonomy is merely a smoke screen for subservience to and domination by the "international establishment." However groundless these suspicions and imputations may be, there is something about the style, the efficiency, the easy "cosmopolitanism," and sometimes the affluence of these agencies that often sets them miles apart—as was of course intended—from the rest of the community. One might even perceive here the elements of a "new class" which is commendably collaborating with agencies like the United Nations or the World Bank to implant efficiency and modernity into the developing country; they could be called the "new comprador class" in contrast to the old-type compradores, that is the local contacts, representatives, and employes of foreign business interests.[14] However admirable this new group may be, its otherness

14. In the same vein, anthropologists have recently identified a "new mestizo" in the Andean countries who acts as a teacher of and spokesman for the Indian, in contrast to the traditional mestizo, cholo, or ladino who has a predominantly exploitative relationship with the Indian. The term "comprador class" is used in the late Paul Baran's *Political Economy of Growth* (Monthly Review, 1957) with the derogatory meaning of local elements who are, because of their economic position, "agents of imperialism."

combined with its close contact with (and always possible escape to) international organizations makes it and the organizations it controls ideal targets for recurrent attacks in the name of nationalism and sovereignty.

Apart from these basic hazards, the autonomous agency device is simply from its birth a rather unstable arrangement. In many cases the élan toward modernity, implicit in the creation of the agency, is short-lived; worse, those who set it up may have been merely paying lip service to the concept because it looked modern or because it was a condition for securing international financial assistance. The statutes through which autonomous agencies are set up usually confer extensive powers upon the board of directors vis-à-vis the government (and upon the general managers vis-à-vis the board). Frequently, then, these statutes are unrealistic; for the government and the board to be genuinely willing to relinquish authority to the extent enunciated in the legal text would imply a degree of change in strongly ingrained habits that is altogether unlikely.

In effect, we see now that the establishment of an autonomous agency does not really confine its trait-making to the *inner* sphere of the newly established activity; by pretending to be "left alone," to make its own appointments and other day-to-day decisions, the agency in effect engages in *generalized trait-making*: it aims at restraining strong appetites and at making over existing and well entrenched attitudes held by the government and the bureaucracy. As in the case of the Damodar Valley Corporation, the attempt to whittle away the autonomy of the agency may start the very day it is born and be carried on unremittingly. In other cases, such as Ethiopia's Imperial Board of Telecommunications, it would be more correct to speak of occasional sharp revolts of the central governmental authority against the discipline it has assumed.

Under the difficult conditions of administrative dualism one must expect such battles between the "modern" agency asserting its rights and the central authorities who are basically unreconciled to the formula to which they have consented in a moment of weakness, passing enthusiasm, or overwhelming desire to get hold of World Bank funds. Conflicts of this kind can actually be character-forming for both parties. Nor does the responsibility for conflict always lie with the central government or the older bureaucracy. Frequently a new agency, deluded by its statute, will misjudge the actual power relationships to such an extent and will act so provocatively toward the older elements in the bureaucracy that it almost asks to forfeit its privileged position. In many of the less developed countries there is a widespread tendency (which explains much of their instability) for everyone to go to the limit of his powers and beyond, and to rely in case of conflict with other power holders on favorable intervention from the very top. In autonomous agencies this tendency is reinforced not only by the statutes that brought them into being but by the reform spirit with which these agencies are often imbued. Their contempt for the old-line bureaucracy and power holders is usually boundless, but it can be reckless as well if it is openly expressed and acted upon, unrestrained by the intimation that administrative dualism, unlike the technological variety, has its breaking point. A visit to the San Lorenzo irrigation project and authority in 1964, exhilarating though it was because of the strong reform wind that was blowing about the place, could not help but generate the uneasy premonition in one visitor that such a breaking point was not very far away.

The preceding discussion is by no means meant as an indictment of the autonomous agency; but in view of the popularity of this device it seemed useful to show that it is not so much an easy way out of the project planners' dilemma between trait-making and trait-taking as a contrivance which, ingenious as it is as an apparent solution, actually incarnates this dilemma in a new form.

CHAPTER FIVE

Project Appraisal:
The Centrality of Side-Effects

OUR DISCUSSION of trait-making and trait-taking implies a new view of a subject usually dealt with under the heading of indirect benefits or side-effects, external economies or benefits, spillovers, linkages, repercussions, and similar terms. It is generally recognized that besides the output of goods and services which is their primary raison d'être, projects have a variety of more subtle, yet perhaps highly important and powerful effects, from the acquisition of new skills to greater readiness, on the part of the consumers of the project's outputs, to produce for the market; from the stimulation of entrepreneurship to the learning of cooperation and discipline; from backward and forward linkages to greater propensity to engage in family planning; from increased literacy to greater confidence in the ability of one's country to achieve progress —not to forget negative effects such as new or heightened social and ethnic tensions, fresh opportunities for spreading corruption, etc. Should and can these multifarious non-output effects of projects be thoroughly canvassed and taken into account in making investment decisions? As one might expect, this question has evoked widely different answers. A short survey of the discussion will be presented below, but first we shall show that much of it can be bypassed as a result of the approach employed in the last chapter.

160

Side-Effects as Essential Requirements

In analyzing the relation between the fortunes of the railways in Nigeria and tribal tensions or corruption, or between the pasture improvement program in Uruguay and the resulting propensity of the landowners to take a greater management interest in their ranches, or between telecommunications in Ethiopia and the spread of the credit system, we were talking about certain indirect effects without mentioning the term. The reason was that these effects did not make their appearance in our discussion as somewhat marginal benefits, as intangible and fuzzy outputs of these various projects, but as factors ("traits") whose presence or absence was required to make the project itself work. Some of the so-called side-effects thus turn out, a bit surprisingly, to be *inputs essential to the realization of the project's principal effect and purpose.*

This conceptual tangle between effects and requirements arises because these inputs or resources (skills, attitudes, propensities) are ordinarily not used up in the production process, either wholly or in part. On the contrary, while some critical minimum amount of such resources is required for the construction or the operation of the project, they increase and spread with and through use so that the resulting increment can then be channeled to new ventures—this is where the side-effect originates. But to justify the need for attention to these resources exclusively by the side-effect would be tantamount to saying that the only reason a pianist should pay attention to playing well during his first recital is that, as a result, he will play even better the next time!

That the discussion of acquisition of new skills and attitudes under the rubric of "indirect benefits" or "side-effects" of projects is topsy-turvy in just this way was forcibly brought home to me by observations in Nigeria and Pakistan which I have already reported. A recent publication argued strongly that in evaluating investment in highways (as an alternative to railways) considerable attention should be given to the indirect benefit consisting in the enhancement of entrepreneurship and upward social mobility that the trucking industry brings with it.[1] Now if the matter is put in this way, one can just see the hard-boiled, no-nonsense transportation economist shrug off this unquantifiable advice and stick to his usual, difficult-enough-as-it-is estimate of transport cost savings, supplemented at most by a forecast of new transportation generated by road or, alternatively, railroad.

It turns out, however, that taking these matters of entrepreneurship into account does not just depend on the *bon plaisir* of the transportation economist. As we have seen, entrepreneurship means political power, which in turn means the ability to change the rules of the transportation game decisively in favor of the highways. This not so meek side-effect, then, does very well at taking care of itself as it becomes reflected in privileges and subsidies enjoyed by highways vis-à-vis railroads (road construction by nonreimbursable public funds, leniency in applying regulations on weight limitation for trucks, etc.). Hence the decision to build a railway must imply some sort of assurance that these innate advantages of the highway-truck complex will not be allowed to nullify the rail investment.

In the case of the Karnaphuli Paper Mill, similarly, a well-meaning project analyst with cross-cultural empathy or sociological leanings might have timidly noted that the building and operation of the mill necessarily involved cooperation between Bengali and non-Bengali Pakistanis; hence, an intangible benefit of the mill, to be added somehow to all the reams of paper it would produce, would consist in the improved relationship between the two human groups whose isolation

1. George W. Wilson *et al.*, *The Impact of Highway Investment on Development* (Brookings Institution, 1966), pp. 195 ff.

from one another and mutual diffidence is one of Pakistan's major problems in consolidating its nationhood. Here again, events revealed that the matter could be put far more forcefully and convincingly: a minimum of mutual toleration and understanding between the two groups was shown to be an essential condition for the very survival of the mill, or at least for the survival of its general manager.

In looking at the so-called secondary benefits one by one, it appears that a large number of them can be transmuted in this fashion into essential inputs. This does not mean that these inputs, once they are successfully in place, do not *also* result in important secondary benefits; but their principal claim to the concentrated attention of project planners lies in their capacity as inputs or, in the language of the preceding chapter, as traits that need to be "made" for the project to function properly. In other words, while their presence brings benefits that are perhaps difficult to evaluate, *their absence inflicts penalties that are anything but nebulous.* This characteristic makes it possible to give at least a partial answer to a question that has become increasingly baffling as more and more side-effects have been discovered—the question "to know where to begin and when to stop."[2] It is clear that one must not stop until he has rounded up and feels reasonably sure which side-effects have this dual input-output quality. The bundle of such side-effects that are also crucially required traits will vary from project to project, and it should be the combined task of engineers and social scientists to identify its composition in each case.

Pure and Mixed Side-Effects

It would be useful to know which side-effects function also (and at times principally) as required or extremely helpful traits and may therefore be termed "mixed" in contrast to

2. Henry Bruton, *Principles of Development Economics* (Prentice-Hall, 1965), p. 293.

those that deserve to be called "pure" side-effects. One reason the required-trait or input quality of so many side-effects has been overlooked may well be that it is either lacking or well concealed in the reinvestment, population, and linkage effects that have been standing in the foreground of the professional discussion. In accordance with the advocates of these effects, projects should not be evaluated only on the basis of the rate of return, but account should also be taken of the differential effects of alternative projects and techniques on the rate of reinvestment, on human fertility, and on entrained industrial and general economic enterprise.[3]

Taking up first the population effect, it is rather clear that it is a "pure" side-effect: the propensity of the producers of the project's outputs or of its consumers or of both to procreate less can hardly be considered essential for the proper functioning of the project (except if the project itself consists in the manufacture of birth control devices, of course).

With respect to reinvestment, the matter is a little more complicated: Ordinarily an increased propensity to invest out of profits, however useful for future growth, could not be considered a requirement for the adequate performance of a project that is already built and in operation. Nonetheless, if the project happens to be in an industry experiencing rapid technological innovation, a high rate of reinvestment will be necessary to keep the industry healthy and competitive. To establish such an industry where profits are largely either consumed or remitted abroad may therefore require some special institutional precaution or care in the selection of partners. To a considerable extent, it may fortunately be expected that the threat of obsolescence and the availability of improved technology which is characteristic of industries where innovation

3. A good survey and general discussion are now available in *ibid.*, pp. 288–95.

is rampant will of itself induce greater reinvestment even in an environment that is not normally accumulation-minded.[4]

If one looks next at backward and forward linkage effects from this viewpoint, it would seem again that these effects, however precious, are not ordinarily required for the proper functioning of the project as such. Forward linkages that increase the demand for the project's outputs will, however, be very useful and in some cases essential for the future growth of the project (they may even be essential for the project as it is, in case the demand estimate the project was based on turns out to be overoptimistic). Backward linkage effects have a similar function: they reduce the import-intensity of the project whose future growth, given the balance-of-payments constraint, may well be conditioned on such a reduction; thus both linkage effects may play an important role in enabling the project to expand, and since the ability to grow is an important attribute of the soundness of a development project, linkage effects qualify after all as mixed side-effects. And as in the case of the reinvestment effect, demand tends to call forth supply: the more the linkage effects are needed for the proper functioning and growth of the project itself, the more likely is their emergence. For example, the more import-intensive an industry, the more likely it is that, with expansion of the industry, some backward linkage effects will assert themselves; it will nevertheless often be desirable to make sure of these effects through various policy measures.

It begins to look, as a result of our discussion so far, as though the "pure" side-effect is a rather rare bird. Certainly all the educational and training effects of projects as well as many of their effects on attitudes, values, institutions, and so-

4. See A. O. Hirschman and Gerald Sirkin, "Investment Criteria and Capital Intensity Once Again," *Quarterly Journal of Economics,* Vol. 72 (August 1958), pp. 469–71.

cial structure are mixed, as our previous examples have demonstrated. Apart from the population effect, pure side-effects may perhaps be found in some of the most "fuzzy" repercussions of development projects, such as the enhanced confidence in their problem-solving ability that may be gained by a country's citizens as a result of a successful project. But other quite general side-effects of projects would again be mixed, as will appear from the following considerations.

In many underdeveloped countries the bureaucracy looks at economic activity, particularly in private commerce and industry, as a potential source of additional short-run gain for itself through more or less extortionist taxation, sale of various required permits, or partnership and other privileges in private enterprise for select officials. Sustained economic development will hardly take root as long as this parasitic behavior of the bureaucracy persists. One possible avenue to the required change may be the deep involvement of a new sector of the bureaucracy in tasks of economic development: in this way a growth- and task-oriented group of public officials may emerge that could eventually do battle with, and perhaps dislodge, the older extortionist group. In this sort of perspective lies a strong justification for the expansion of the public sector in an underdeveloped economy; in fact, if this expansion were to be instrumental in changing the bureaucracy from self-serving to public-serving,[5] from extortionist to growth-oriented, then it would be very much in the interests of the long-suffering private sec-

5. The difference between Western and non-Western bureaucracies is discussed in terms of these concepts in a stimulating unpublished paper by Nadav Safran who, however, sees the emergence of public-serving bureaucracies in the West as resulting from the chastening experience these bureaucracies underwent in the nineteenth century when they saw their role strictly confined and their attributes narrowly circumscribed. Since this experience seems unlikely to be duplicated elsewhere, it is tempting to speculate whether a similar transformation could result from the opposite movement—an expansion in the role of the bureaucracies.

tor itself. At the same time, such a change in the character of the bureaucracy would be a most impressive side-effect of development projects in the public sector.

The indicated sequence will obviously not result from just any involvement of the government in additional economic activities, and we cannot attempt to analyze here the conditions under which a traditionally parasitic bureaucracy's venture into construction and operation of development projects will change its character.[6] The possibility that such a sequence may occur is, however, suggested by events in several underdeveloped areas:[7] among our projects, the remarkable career of Thailand's Royal Irrigation Department (RID) provides a good approximation to the model we have sketched. The department itself, the Yanhee Electricity Authority, and the other enterprises that RID has promoted are recognized as remarkable instances of dynamic entrepreneurship and efficient management in the public sector, in marked contrast to the fumbling and "milking" approach of some official Thai ventures in manufacturing.[8]

The successes and the drive of RID have strengthened the agency's position within the government over the years, as was indicated, for example, by the appointment in 1964 of its longtime director and guiding spirit, Xujati Kambhu, to the post of Deputy Minister of National Development. In this manner,

6. Our discussion of latitudes (Chap. 3) and of trait-making in relation to latitude or lack of latitude (Chap. 4) has of course many implications for such an analysis.

7. The emergence of an efficient, growth-oriented group of public officials in an otherwise miasmic bureaucratic environment is perceptively analyzed for the case of electric power in Brazil by Judith D. Tendler, *The Rise of Public Power in Brazil* (to be published in 1968 by Harvard University Press), Chap. 6.

8. See Fred W. Riggs, *Thailand: The Modernization of a Bureaucratic Policy* (East-West Center, 1966), Chap. 10; and Robert J. Muscat, *Development Strategy in Thailand* (Praeger, 1966), Chap. 4.

the achievements of RID may contribute to a firmer commitment of the Thai bureaucracy as a whole to the objective of long-term economic growth.

Here, then, is a very general, fairly uncertain, yet potentially most significant "side-effect" of a project (or of a series of projects). And, once again, this effect is mixed rather than pure, in the sense that it is also required for the proper functioning and growth of the project itself. For without some modification of the bureaucracy's traditional exploitative approach toward economic activity, the expanding undertakings of the Royal Irrigation Department would have bogged down as a result of penetration by parasitic elements, and the organization could never have gone on to the many new tasks, both in irrigation and other sectors, it has successfully shouldered.

Our conclusion is that there are hardly any "pure" side-effects. Important side-effects are likely to be mixed—that is, they will be essential or valuable inputs as well as intangible outputs. Attention must therefore be paid to them by the project analyst, not only for the purpose of evaluating their benefits, but mainly to make sure of them for the sake of the success and mere survival of the project itself.

Smuggling in Change via Side-Effects

Thus far we have not addressed ourselves directly to the question usually asked in connection with indirect benefits or side-effects: "Should these benefits or effects influence the choice between alternative investment projects, alongside the rate of return?"

We staved off answering this question by taking up another one: "Should attention be paid to these effects?" This question at first looks like a shorthand, somewhat vaguely worded version of the longer one. But by showing that the side-effects are most of the time performing also as factors, traits, or inputs essential or valuable for the proper functioning of the project itself, we were able to deal with the latter question on its own terms and to answer it with a resounding "yes" without taking a position on the former question. Attention must be paid to these effects, we found, not so much because they may affect the ranking of projects in the rather hypothetical situation when different projects with varying rates of return and side-effects come up simultaneously for decision, but because they often are the very stuff of project design, success, and failure.

One observation may be added here. We often apprehend, so it would seem, these factors and traits more easily as effects than as conditions; in other words, by focusing on the possible effects of projects, we discover additional requirements of success. This is so because they are often, as we have seen, *eventual* requirements, essential if the project is to endure and to flourish, but not needed from the start. Hence, a search for the indirect effects is to be recommended if only as a heuristic device, as a means of identifying some of the basic conditions for the project's success.

We are now ready to take up the question whether side-effects should be counted in investment decisions so that they could occasionally modify or override decisions based solely on rate-of-return considerations. After the previous discussion, one is immediately tempted to turn in a strongly positive reply. The chapter on trait-making (the Nigerian railway example, in particular) has shown how revolutionary some projects would have to be in their effects on social structure, attitudes, skills, etc. in order to be successful and how easily and seriously they run into trouble because built-in revolutionary implications have remained unnoticed—is it not right then that they should get full credit for such side-effects when they are successful? But rather than allow ourselves to be swayed in this complex matter by elementary feelings of justice, we should first give the opposition a hearing.[9]

The principal way of warding off the intrusion of indirect effects in project appraisal has long been to point out that the desirable indirect effects or by-products of projects could ordinarily become available as the *direct* effects or *principal* products of other types of activities such as education, taxation, administration, the political process, etc. For example, why bother to evaluate the differential impact of projects on the birthrate when over-population can be directly attacked through an active birth control policy? Why make reinvestment of profits rather than simply profits an important consideration of project selection when appropriate tax policy can presumably achieve a commanding influence on reinvestment policies? Why worry about the effect of an irrigation project on land tenure and land reform when the latter is clearly a matter of changing the country's basic property patterns through central political processes, be they legal or revolutionary?[10]

9. It is of course assumed that a conscientious effort is made to compute side-effects for *all* projects that compete for funds. In practice this rule is frequently violated by advocates who claim considerable indirect benefits for *their* project but do not inquire into corresponding advantages of competing projects. It goes without saying that unless side-effects are evaluated for all projects, it would be better to have investment decisions proceed on the basis of direct benefits alone. See also below, p. 178.

10. This is, on the whole, the position of Bruton, *Principles of Development Economics*, pp. 288–95. For an early expression of this point of view in connection with the discussion around the Galenson-Leibenstein thesis on investment criteria (W. Galenson and H. Leibenstein, "Investment Criteria, Productivity and Economic Development," *Quarterly Journal of Economics*, Vol. 69 [August 1955], pp. 343–70), see the papers by John Moes and H. H. Villard in *Quarterly Journal of Economics*, Vol. 71 (February and August 1957), pp. 462–70, and the effective reply by Galenson and Leibenstein on pp. 473–74.

The answers to such questions cannot be dogmatic. They must be given on the basis of one's best estimates (a) of the strength of the side-effect, and (b) of the likelihood that independent action will actually be taken to achieve the above noted ends directly. Suppose, in relation to the last two questions, that the chances are not good for appropriate fiscal or land reform policies to be forthcoming: then, if certain projects can either substitute for official inaction or act as a spur to official action, they should be greatly prized and earn some special rating for behaving in this way.

We are here touching on a noneconomic, but nonetheless important, reason why indirect effects may be neglected in advanced countries without undue risk, but must be closely watched and capitalized on in the underdeveloped world.[11] In the former, with interests fully articulated and political functions actively performed by agencies and organs set up for this purpose, it is perhaps legitimate to expect that every man, from legislator to educator, from planner to policeman, will do his duty. In such a "Nelsonian" world the project analyst can, like everyone else, stick to *his* last, that is, just worry about the rate of return. But to do so in an underdeveloped environment would mean to *assume away that very environment,* which is definitely non-Nelsonian. Here, on the contrary, essential functions frequently are performed, if at all, in unexpected fashion, that is, by parties not normally assigned to performing them.

In another connection, we have drawn the distinction between privileged problems (for example, inflation and balance-of-payments pressures) that catch the policy maker's attention and neglected problems (for example, land reform) that in the past often had to ride the coattails of the privileged ones.[12]

11. See note 18, p. 177 for a similar, but more narrowly economic argument.
12. See *Journeys Toward Progress,* pp. 229–35.

Where policies directed toward improved taxation, administration, birth control, land reform, etc. often find it difficult to develop enough of their "own" power, the art of coattail riding is obviously very useful. And certain projects lend themselves particularly well to being ridden on, for various reasons.

In the first place, a project may be useful as a device to make acceptable, and even palatable, changes that would be rejected if they were proposed in pure form, unalloyed with the compensating advantages a project carries with it. Just as the policy makers' eagerness to solve the privileged problem makes them more inclined to look at the neglected problem that, so they have been told, lies at the root of the privileged one, so their overwhelming desire to harness a river or to build up a telecommunications network may make them accept administrative arrangements or training programs or rate policies that would never be adopted in isolation.

Another and far more significant variety of coattail riding occurs when social, institutional, or attitudinal changes are not explicitly acquiesced in or adopted along with the project from the start, but emerge slowly from the workings of the project. The better known indirect effects such as the acquisition of skills and linkages belong in this category. So do of course the more recherché entrained changes with which we have become acquainted, from the Uruguayan landlord who turns from absentee to "presentee," to the replacement of cash by credit transaction as a result of long-distance telephone communications in Ethiopia.

In some of these cases, it is conceivable that the project would not have been undertaken if the decision makers had fully visualized all of its consequences. For example, the San Lorenzo irrigation project would hardly have been started in the early 1950's in Peru if it had been anticipated that the project would one day become a training and testing ground for agrarian reform. Here social change was smuggled in, as it were, along with the project. To some extent all projects have this Trojan Horse quality, because they always bring many unanticipated changes beyond their immediate and expected physical and production accomplishments.

In the light of these observations, the refusal to take side-effects into consideration at the moment of project appraisal could be reinterpreted to mean just the opposite of hostility and contempt; it could spring from greatest solicitude and affection for these effects coupled with concern lest indiscreet prying into the remoter consequences of projects may do more harm than good by putting an end to this flourishing and beneficial smuggling in of change that goes on under the guise of putting up development projects.

As this argument is strongly reminiscent of the Hiding Hand, we do not wish to disavow it entirely. It may have considerable validity in countries where any sort of change is greatly feared and resisted. Nevertheless, there is little need to worry that analysts will ever detect all the changes that are likely to be entrained by a project. Happily for the smuggling-in act, the changes that are most subversive of the existing order are often hardest to detect for the simple reason that the more fundamental the change, the more ramified and hence innocuous-looking will be its beginnings. What de Tocqueville says about the French Revolution—"Never has there been a set of events that was greater in import, longer in gestation, more thorough in preparation, and less foreseen"—is likely to hold for fundamental social transformation in general. Hence, the project-entrained changes which, if detected, would make the existing power holders think twice before authorizing a project will often slip through their net.

On the other hand, there are today more and more countries in which the subtle modernizing changes a project brings with it no longer need to be smuggled in, but would on the contrary be greatly welcomed. Making it clear that the project serves as carrier for these desired changes would therefore result in speedier and more energetic action.

Finally it must be recalled that side-effects can be negative as well as positive. A project can spread corruption just as well as it can teach skills, discipline, and achievement motivation; it can increase social tension, exacerbate regional or ethnic jealousies, or lead to considerable disenchantment and frustration because of the exaggerated expectations with which it was launched and of the political and administrative problems it encounters on its way.[13] Spelling out the probabilities of such unwelcome side-effects could lead to a modification of the investment decision or at least to giving the project in question a lower priority rating.

Cost-Benefit Analysis and the Offensive Against Side-Effects

Having stated the general case for taking side-effects into account in project decisions, we must pursue the argument into the somewhat more specialized domain of cost-benefit analysis. This subject area could be cited as a classical example of lack of communication, not between two cultures or even two disciplines, but between two branches of the same discipline.[14] On the one hand, there is a sizable literature dealing with cost-benefit analysis, primarily in developed countries, that with virtual unanimity takes a highly critical view of the very notion

13. The disruptive and destabilizing effects of economic development have recently received increased attention. See Samuel P. Huntington, "Political Development and Political Decay," *World Politics*, Vol. 17 (April 1965), especially pp. 405 ff.; Mancur Olson, "Rapid Growth as a Destabilizing Force," *Journal of Economic History*, Vol. 27 (December 1963), pp. 529–52.

14. See also Timothy King, "Development Strategy and Investment Criteria: Complementary or Competitive?" *Quarterly Journal of Economics*, Vol. 80 (February 1966), pp. 108–20.

of secondary benefits; on the other, in the literature of economic development, the voices pointing up the importance of such effects have become increasingly strong.

Our attempt at establishing communication will start with a brief review of the former group of writings. The discussion of indirect or secondary benefits got underway in the United States in connection with the appraisal of irrigation projects. Because of the widely different and often exaggerated claims staked by advocates of competing projects, the Bureau of Reclamation felt a need to develop uniform standards for the assessment of indirect benefits of projects. According to the Bureau's Reclamation Manual of 1952, such benefits included principally: (1) the "stemming benefits," or the net value added through subsequent handling, processing, and marketing to the farm output that is due to irrigation; and (2) the "induced benefits," or the profits made by enterprises supplying goods and services to the project either for family living or for purposes of agricultural production (for example, fertilizer and farm machinery).

To make precise calculation possible, the manual supplied percentages to be applied to the various farm outputs for the stemming benefits and to the farm and family purchases for the induced benefits. For example, the percentages for the stemming benefits ranged from 6 percent for poultry products to 83 percent for cotton, the difference reflecting the degree of processing required before these products reach the final consumer. The many arbitrary assumptions underlying these figures provided any would-be critic with a tempting target. But the criticism that ensued not only ridiculed this misguided, if heroic, attempt at quantification; it went on to attack the very concept of secondary benefits and to deny their existence.

The barrage was started almost simultaneously by Margolis, Eckstein, and McKean, and their arguments were backed by later writers.[15] The principal line of argument has been that the existence of stemming and induced benefits is predicated on the presence of either general unemployment or of pockets of regional unemployment due to factor immobility. In other words, allowance for indirect benefits reflects the multiplier approach to investment characteristic of depression economics which is out of place in benefit-cost analysis whose "basic assumption is that the investment in natural resources is made in a framework of economic stability and of steady growth" as well as in "the absence of wide departures from economic balance."[16] The principal argument against "counting" induced or stemming benefits is that, with full employment, a marginal displacement of resources toward the project site (to help ridicule the argument, one generally picks barbershops as an example) is not going to produce a net increase in the social product since, with the assumption of stability and steady growth, these resources would otherwise be employed elsewhere. Under the stipulated conditions, the project's direct benefits, valued at market prices, fully reflect its social benefits.

The critics' only qualification of this argument is in the evaluation of a project from the point of view of the region in which it is to be situated. While from the nation's point of

15. Otto Eckstein, *Water Resource Development: The Economics of Project Evaluation* (Harvard University Press, 1958), particularly pp. 206–18; Roland N. McKean, *Efficiency in Government through Systems Analysis with Emphasis on Water Resource Development* (Wiley, 1958), particularly Chap. 9; J. Margolis, "Secondary Benefits, External Economics and the Justification of Public Investment," *Review of Economics and Statistics* (August 1957), pp. 284–91; J. Hirshleifer, J. C. DeHaven, and J. W. Milliman, *Water Supply: Economics, Technology, and Policy* (University of Chicago Press, 1960), particularly pp. 126–36; Arthur Maass et al., *Design of Water Resource Systems* (Harvard University Press, 1962), particularly the section by S. Marglin, pp. 221–27. Eckstein (pp. 202 ff.) and McKean (pp. 154 ff.) give accounts of Bureau of Reclamation practices.

16. Eckstein, *Water Resource Development*, p. 212.

view the increase in miscellaneous economic activities attracted by the project to that region is offset, in conditions of
full employment, by a decline elsewhere, this decline need not
be taken into account when the benefit of a project to its own
region is computed. However, to take this local or regional
point of view rather than the national one is then easily shown
to be irrational, at least in the absence of the most compelling
arguments for geographical balance.

It is perhaps sufficient to have sketched the reasoning that
has caused modern cost-benefit analysis as developed in and
for the United States to dismiss the concept of secondary benefits in order to realize that this conclusion is wholly untransferable to less fortunate economic climes.[17] In less developed
countries it is impossible to assume steady growth, full employment, or perfect mobility of people and capital. Development projects in these countries have precisely the mission to
reduce prevailing unemployment and underemployment, to
absorb immobile factors of production, and, in general, to
ignite growth sequences rather than merely to step, as it were,
on an already fast-moving escalator.[18] This is so well recognized that nobody has ever tried to apply the devastating
Eckstein-McKean critique of the concepts of induced and
stemming benefits to their blood brothers, namely to the back-

17. This is fully recognized by Eckstein at the end of his book, p. 280.
18. The above arguments for and against the inclusion of indirect
benefits in the benefit-cost calculus is very similar to the more general
debate on side-effects presented on pp. 170–74. Eckstein, McKean, *et al.*
essentially argue in terms of an environment in which functions are both
highly specialized and efficiently performed so that someone else can be
expected to be looking out for full employment, steady growth, factor
mobility, etc. Hence the project analyst can safely concentrate on direct
costs and benefits and can neglect the project's positive or negative contribution to wider economic policy objectives. The counter-argument is that,
insofar as less developed countries are concerned, the above "Nelsonian"
expectation (that every man will do his duty) is wholly unwarranted and
that the project carries and must assume a far greater burden.

ward and forward linkage effects, respectively, that I proposed
at just about the same time as important guides to investment
decisions in underdeveloped countries.[19] On the contrary,
backward and forward linkages have become widely accepted
as useful concepts in the analysis of the process of industrialization and in the weighing of priorities for sectors, subsectors,
and projects.

There are two additional reasons why the linkage concept
has fared rather well in comparison to the stemming and induced benefits. In the first place, I proposed it as a general tool
of industrial investment planning, applicable alike to the public and private sectors, while the stemming and induced benefits were proposed only in connection with public water
resource projects. Such a partial approach runs into the elementary objection that any method of estimating benefits additional to the direct ones must be applied uniformly to all sectors and projects competing for available investment funds;
otherwise misallocation of scarce capital resources will surely
result. This objection can be overcome either by taking indirect benefits into account in the evaluation of all other projects, public and private, or by disregarding them in water
projects. The latter course was advocated by the critics for the
reasons already explained, but partly also because the concept
of stemming and induced benefits suffered discredit from the
outset because of the partial way in which it was put forward.

Another reason for the comparative success of the linkage
concept may be that, unlike the Bureau of Reclamation, I did
not try to make these indirect benefits additive to the direct
benefits; it was this attempt that led the Bureau to specify the
battery of percentages for stemming, induced, and other indirect benefits that lent itself so well to ridicule. While I pro-

19. *Strategy of Economic Development,* Chap. 6. Eckstein's, Mc-
Kean's, and my book were all published in 1958.

posed a procedure for making a quantitative estimate of linkage effects, particularly the backward variety, I never thought it possible nor even desirable to amalgamate all the considerations that should go into the making of investment decisions into a single figure.

The quest for a unique ranking device probably accounts for the hostility of economists toward side-effects and secondary benefits. Yet this quest is clearly futile. How could it be expected that it is possible to rank development projects along a single scale by amalgamating all their varied dimensions into a single index when far simpler, everyday choices require the use of individual or collective judgment in the weighing of alternative objectives and in the trade-off between them? There is much to be said, it is true, for facilitating decision making by reducing the many aspects of a project to a few crucial characteristics, one of which would of course be the rate of return.[20] It is one thing to permit, in this way, the decision maker to use informed judgment in making critical choices and trade-offs; it is quite another, however, for the technician to aim at dispensing with such judgment altogether.

20. The rate of return (or, if that is preferred, the present value of the project) results itself from a heroic compression of all the financial data—prospective costs and benefits—into a single figure, and as always with such statistical expressions, some valuable and important aspects of reality are lost in the process. Take, for example, two projects with the same rate, but where one experiences slowly increasing benefits while the other shows at first high returns which then drop off rapidly in the later years. While rate of return calculations imply uniform reinvestment behavior (all returns are presumed to be reinvested at the same internal rate of return), different time shapes of profits are in fact likely to have an important differential influence on reinvestment behavior and on other policies of the project managers, such as expenditures for research and development, for training, etc. This is not an argument against computing the rate of return, but for looking at the time shape of returns as a source of important indirect effects that need to be recorded alongside the rate of return.

This aim would be implicit in the submission of a one-dimensional scale to a then obsolete "decision maker." The technician's dictatorial ambition is often strangely combined with his disclaimer of responsibility for the ultimate decision which he shrugs off as having been influenced by "political" factors. Political is here equated with irrational, if not worse; the heavy price for the unique ranking is in fact that, with many important considerations excluded from the technicians' purview, the decision maker will in the end make more rather than less use of his intuition and "seat-of-the-pants" judgment than if the technicians had set themselves the more modest goal of comparing projects according to a limited number of criteria. Thus, by his ambition to usurp, through the unique ranking device, the political decision maker's essential weighing function, the technician may in effect encourage irresponsible decision making.[21]

Counteroffensives

In turning to the treatment of indirect effects in the literature of economic development, I have singled out backward and

21. In a rather similar vein, Arthur Maass has protested recently against the idea "that the professional planners should design projects and programs for economic efficiency, for which benefit-cost analysis can provide the necessary ranking function; and that thereafter these project designs can be doctored and modified by a political process to account for any 'uneconomic' objectives." Maass objects to this practice for the excellent reason that "where government programs are intended for complex objectives they should be designed, where this is possible, for such objectives, not designed for one objective, which may not be the most important, and subsequently modified to take account of others." See "Benefit-Cost Analysis: Its Relevance to Public Investment Decisions," *Quarterly Journal of Economics*, Vol. 80 (May 1966), p. 214. According to Maass, the planners should spell out the possible trade-offs between the efficiency and other objectives; he cites some examples from United States programs in highways and housing to show that some necessary choices can be made rationally through political processes.

forward linkages not because I have a proprieta.y interest in them, but because of their unnoticed, yet close connection with the induced and stemming benefits that gave rise to the onslaught against secondary benefits in the literature already quoted. After this demonstration of what I called before lack of communication between two branches of the same discipline, a brief survey of the trend of thinking on indirect effects of economic activities as factors in economic development is in order.

To a considerable extent, the recent interest in this matter is a rediscovery of a once well worked terrain: the differential effects of economic activities on human skills, on institutions, and on such matters as probity and punctuality were a lively concern of the classical economists.[22] The current discussion started with the natural question whether the international division of labor between industrial countries and those specializing in exporting foodstuffs and raw materials had perhaps something to do with the sustained progress of the former and the retardation of the latter. In 1949 Singer called attention to the positive effects of manufacturing on "the general level of education, skill, way of life, inventiveness, habits, store of technology, creation of new demand, etc."[23] With the subject thus newly opened up for discussion, it was soon realized that the significant differences between the indirect effects of economic activities could not be formulated so broadly, since cumulative growth could be shown to have resulted from agricultural expansion in some countries while others fell short of this achievement in spite of incipient industrialization.

22. Nathan Rosenberg, "Neglected Dimensions in the Analysis of Economic Change," Oxford Bulletin, Vol. 26, No. 1 (1964), particularly pp. 62–66.

23. H. W. Singer, "The Distribution of Gains between Investing and Borrowing Countries," reprinted in his International Development: Growth and Change (McGraw-Hill, 1964), p. 164.

Attempts were therefore soon made to move away from the grand, but sterile agriculture-industry dichotomy. This could be done by making side-effects depend on certain general characteristics that are present in all productive processes to a greater or smaller extent. Naturally enough, the characteristics first fastened on as possible sources of important indirect benefits were traditional categories of economic analysis: capital intensity and the propensity to save out of income. Plausibly it was suggested that high capital-labor ratios are likely to have a stimulating effect, as already noted, on reinvestment out of profits; a rather more tenuous hypothesis was that capital intensity would help dampen population growth.[24] The argument was later extended to the again rather convincing idea that, because of the nature of production functions and of technical progress, high capital-labor ratios are peculiarly conducive to the rapid incorporation of technological innovations.[25]

These propositions about the plentiful positive side-effects of capital intensity are helpful in understanding the acceleration of industrial growth in countries where capital-intensive industry is already an important part of the economic scene. The technological portion of the argument was in fact specifically devised for this purpose. Unfortunately, these insights are rather less useful for capital-poor, "pre-take-off" countries looking for economic activities with favorable effects; for to hand these countries the advice to develop capital-intensive industries is rather like counseling a young man from a poor family who is starting out in life to find himself a wealthy grandfather.

24. Galenson and Leibenstein, in *Quarterly Journal of Economics*.
25. H. Leibenstein, "Technical Progress, the Production Function, and Development," in W. W. Rostow (ed.), *The Economics of Take-Off into Sustained Growth* (St. Martin's, 1963), pp. 185–200.

A similar critique can be made of another, almost simultaneous effort to identify, this time within agriculture, differential growth impulses yielded by various types of productive activities. Here again, favorable and unfavorable effects on further economic growth were derived from economic characteristics such as factor intensities and saving propensities, suitably combined with some institutional assumptions about newly settled regions. The result was not too surprising: crops that require the large-scale, labor-intensive plantation were shown to be less propitious for sustained economic advance than agricultural pursuits that lend themselves to being carried on by family-size farm units. Among other effects, the latter arrangement leads to a more equitable distribution of income and therefore permits the setting up of manufactures to serve the local market at an earlier stage than does the plantation economy. Once again, then, it was shown that it paid to be "modern."[26]

The next attempt at formulating general criteria for the identification of crucial side-effects was probably my own. The backward and forward linkage concepts were supposed to result in a ranking of economic activities in accordance with their igniting potential.

One of the best established side-effects of industry and new economic activity in general is the acquisition of skills. In recent years, moreover, interest in education and "human capital" as important factors in explaining growth has multiplied. No general attempt has been made to rank industries according to the extent to which they impart new skills or are conducive to the acquisition of new abilities, but elements for

---

26. R. E. Baldwin, "Patterns of Development in Newly Settled Regions," *Manchester School of Economics and Social Studies*, Vol. 24 (May 1956), pp. 161–79. The complementary nature of the Galenson-Leibenstein and the Baldwin analyses has not been sufficiently noted.

such a ranking begin to be available. The lack of cumulative economic growth in several African countries, in spite of their success in developing cash crops such as cocoa, coffee, peanuts, etc. for export, has been explained by the fact that these economic activities, though new, failed to act as agents of qualitative change of the agricultural labor force.[27] At the opposite pole we have the machine tool industry with its peculiar ability to develop "new skills and techniques . . . in response to the demands of specific customers" and to act as "the main transmission center for the transfer of new skills and techniques to the entire machine-using center of the economy."[28] Unfortunately, all of these examples seem to take us back once again to the agriculture-industry dichotomy or to the sort of unhelpful advice—take a big jump and become capital- or machine-tool-intensive or otherwise advanced—that we were trying to get away from. It must be admitted here that by itself the linkage concept had led me to take up similarly unhelpful positions.[29]

It may seem strange that one reaches so similar and by now rather unexciting results no matter how he slices up the array of industries or economic activities under consideration. The

27. Hla Myint, "An Interpretation of Economic Backwardness" (1954), reprinted in A. N. Agarwala and S. P. Singh (eds.), *The Economics of Underdevelopment* (Oxford University Press, 1958), pp. 119–213; R. E. Baldwin, "Export Technology and Development from a Subsistence Level," *Economic Journal*, Vol. 73 (March 1963), pp. 80–92.

28. Nathan Rosenberg, "Technological Change in the Machine Tool Industry," *Journal of Economic History*, Vol. 23 (December 1963), pp. 414–43. In a subsequent, unpublished paper Rosenberg identifies another growth-promoting characteristic of the machine tool industry: the fact that complex machine tools are generally replete with imbalances—there are always some parts capable of performing at a higher rate than some bottleneck components toward which efforts at technological improvement are thus compellingly oriented. It is not clear, however, whether this internal imbalance is more prominent in the machine tool industry than in other industries or whether it is less well tolerated there because of the special, restless turn of mind of the people in that industry.

29. *Strategy of Economic Development*, pp. 109–10.

explanation lies perhaps in the method common to the various approaches here described. It consists in identifying some, supposedly crucial, characteristic in which all or the most important beneficial side-effects are said to originate. How is such a characteristic or criterion to be found? By taking a good look at the most dynamic activities of the advanced countries and by picking out some quality that abounds in these activities. Little wonder then that an application of the resulting criterion will lead one right back to these activities as the most desirable ones, and to activities typical of underdeveloped countries as the least blessed with indirect benefits. Here lies the simple explanation for the convergence of the various criteria, at least for the "best" economic activities, toward the same sort of highly advanced industries or pursuits and also for the fact that they are so much less revealing than one might have hoped.

I have no wish to deprecate unduly the various criteria; they are likely to be quite useful in those middle ranges between the "best" and "worst" activities that are often truly relevant to the investment decisions in developing countries. Here, they should be able to supplement rate-of-return considerations in identifying particularly promising ventures. In these ranges, of course, the criteria are much less likely to coincide in the manner they do for their extreme values, and their divergent indications could pose difficult, but highly significant and important problems for the decision maker who on occasion may face a choice between one project that is long on linkages, but short on training effects, and another that has the opposite characteristics.

Modesty and Ambition in Project Planning

The outcome of the discussion of indirect effects may appear to be puzzling or frustrating: on the one hand, I have stressed the importance of these effects; on the other, I have given at

most two cheers for the various criteria that have been proposed to identify and to measure them. The reason for this
lukewarm endorsement is my conviction, based on the field
survey of project histories, that the indirect effects are so varied
as to escape detection by one or even several criteria *uniformly
applied to all projects*. Upon inspection, each project turns
out to represent a *unique constellation* of experiences and
consequences, of direct and indirect effects. This uniqueness
in turn results from the varied interplay between the structural
characteristics of projects, on the one hand, and the social and
political environment, on the other. To facilitate the understanding of this interplay I focused in the earlier chapters of
this essay on various properties of projects—primarily uncertainties and latitudes—that condition their *total* behavior and
career, that is, their productive performance no less than their
contribution, positive or negative, to a variety of ulterior tasks.
There was no intention to erect these manifold aspects of
project behavior into full-fledged criteria that should be applied to all projects; rather I was seeking to provide project
planners and operators with a large set of glasses with which to
discern probable lines of project behavior, in the expectation
that the analysis of each individual project would require
different and rather limited subsets of the full set of glasses
which has been exhibited.

Two essential and distinctive features of this approach
should be noted. First, it takes its criteria wherever they are
to be found, whether among the available and traditional categories of economic analysis or among technical, administrative,
and any other project characteristics that can be shown to have
significant effects on project behavior.

Secondly, it attempts to identify significant *events* and *problems* that are likely to mark the project's path, whereas the
criteria for indirect benefits which have been reviewed address
themselves solely to those aspects (training effects, linkages,

etc.) that could be unequivocally classified as *qualities* or as corresponding *defects* of projects. It is probably this orientation that so restricts the usefulness of these criteria, for a very large part of a project's career is made up of events that, as we have repeatedly stressed, cannot be classified neatly into these two opposed categories.

As a last illustration take the case of the San Lorenzo irrigation project. It might have been foreseen that a structural characteristic of irrigation projects—namely, the limited amount of water that was going to be made available—would lead to a conflict between the established group of plantation owners in the Lower Piura Valley and the new agency intent on encouraging new types of diversified agriculture and land tenure. Is this good or bad? In other words, should the project have received a specially high priority on this account or, on the contrary, should it perhaps have been eschewed? It is obviously impossible to answer this question without developing some opinion and hunches about the probable course of the conflict, its outcome for the parties directly concerned, and its effect on socioeconomic development of Peru in general.

A prospective event of this kind may therefore be adjudged to be beneficial in one set of circumstances, pernicious in another. Elsewhere I have shown that many so-called obstacles to development do not seem to perform as such in some situations and even turn out, in others, to act as blessings in disguise.[30] Some of the most characteristic and significant events in the career of projects are ambiguous in this way, and the decision whether to give them a positive or a negative sign in the course of project appraisal requires considerable knowledge of the country no doubt, but also—and this is what I have

30. "Obstacles to Development: A Classification and a Quasi-Vanishing Act," *Economic Development and Cultural Change*, Vol. 13 (July 1965), pp. 385–93.

been trying to convey—an awareness of the ways in which projects create entirely new openings for change.

Earlier I argued in favor of abandoning the search for a ranking device that would presume to aggregate the direct and indirect effects of projects. It is now seen that the project analyst must be still more modest: he cannot even pretend to classify uniformly, for purposes of decision making, the various properties and probable lines of behavior of projects, as either advantages or drawbacks, benefits or costs, assets or liabilities. But this modesty with respect to generalized evaluation and quantification is in reality the necessary counterpart of the large and free-swinging ambitions projects must entertain and cultivate in countries where they are called upon to make a contribution to progress that goes far beyond their immediate production tasks. That projects are felt to be endowed with that sort of ambitious mission was clearly apparent from the personalities and outlook of the men in charge of the more successful projects I visited.

Much remains to be done in understanding the conditions for failure and success of projects—and, in general, of new economic activities—within this wider setting. I hope to have provided for this purpose, as a result of close observation of actual project behavior, some useful principles of classification and analysis. This is my version of Kolakowski's "tiny waterhole" which I am glad to settle for after having pursued in these pages what could only be a mirage—the snatching of systematic insight from casual hindsight.

Index

Index

191